MW00763189

INCORPORATING IN NEVADA

INCORORATING IN NEVADA

How Anyone, Anywhere, Can Enjoy Tax Savings, Liability Protection, and Privacy

THIRD EDITION
**A STEP BY STEP GUIDE
TO INCORPORATING YOUR
BUSINESS IN NEVADA**

Cort W. Christie

Incorporator of over 10,000 corporations

Griffin Publishing Group
Torrance, California

© 2001 by Cort W. Christie

This publication is a creative work fully protected by all applicable rights. All rights reserved. No portion of this book may be reproduced or transmitted in any form or by any means, electronic or mechanical, including fax, photocopy, recording, or any information storage or retrieval system by anyone except the purchaser for his or her own use.

DIRECTOR OF OPERATIONS: Robin L. Howland

PROJECT MANAGER: Bryan K. Howland

BOOK DESIGN: m2design group

PROOFREADER: Mark Davis

COVER DESIGN: Arnold Lopez

10 9 8 7 6 5 4 3 2 1

ISBN 1-58000-077-0

While a great deal of care has been taken to provide accurate information, the ideas, suggestions, general principles, and conclusions presented in this publication are subject to local, state, and federal laws and regulations, court cases, and any revisions of same. The reader is thus urged to consult legal counsel regarding any points of law discussed herein. This publication should not be used as a substitute for competent legal advice.

This material is intended to provide accurate and authoritative information with regard to the subject matter covered. It is offered with the understanding that the publisher is not engaged in rendering legal, accounting, or other professional services. If legal advice or other expert assistance is required, the services of a competent professional person should be retained.

From the declaration of principles jointly adopted by a committee of the American Bar Association and a committee of Publishers and Associates.

Griffin Publishing Group
2908 Oregon Court, Suite I-5
Torrance, CA 90503
Phone: (310) 381-0485
Fax: (310) 381-0499

Manufactured in the United States of America

TABLE OF CONTENTS

ACKNOWLEDGEMENTS IX

INTRODUCTION XI

1 THE PERILS OF BUSINESS
   Litigation 2
   Taxes 3

2 WHICH BUSINESS STRUCTURE IS RIGHT FOR YOU?
   Entity Comparison Chart 5
   Sole Proprietorships 6
   General Partnerships 7
   Limited Partnerships 8
   Limited Liability Companies 9

3 CORPORATIONS...WHICH ONE?
   Businesses Taxed as a Corporation 14
   "C" versus "S" 15
   "S" Corporations 16
   "C" Corporations 17
   Private vs. Public Corporations 17
   Closely Held Corporations 18
   Domestic Corporations. 18
   Foreign Corporations 18
   Alien Corporations 19
   Nonprofit Corporations 19
   Personal Holding Corporations 20
   Personal Service Corporations 20
   Holding Corporations 21

4 CORPORATIONS STILL #1
   Why Incorporate? 23
   Individual vs. Corporation 23
   Liability Protection. 24
   Asset Protection 25
   Tax Savings 26

Raising Capital 27
Reducing Audit Risk 28
Living the Corporate Lifestyle 28
Building Credit 29
Estate Planning 29
Corporate Image 29
Corporate Advantage 30

5 THE CORPORATION HAVEN: NEVADA

History of Nevada Corporations 31
What Nevada Case Law Says. 33
14 Facts That Make Nevada Corporation's Shield Ultra Strong 34
Comparison of State Statutes 36
Piercing the Corporate Veil 36
How Nevada Is Becoming #1 in Incorporation Services 37
No Need to Come to Nevada 40

6 LIVE AND WORK ANYWHERE YOU WANT BUT INCORPORATING IN NEVADA IS A MUST

Anyone Can Form a Nevada Corporation 41
A Nevada Based Corporation 42
What a Nevada Corporation Takes With It Across State Borders 42
When Will Nevada Law Apply Outside Its Borders 43

7 CREATIVE CORPORATIONS

Privacy Strategies. 45
Tax Savings. 46
Home State Corporation Strategies 48
Financing 49
Tax Savings Plan 49
Judgment Proofing Yourself and the Corporation 50
Security Agreements 52
Nontaxable Exchange of Property 53
Real Estate in Another State 56
Protecting Personal Savings 56
Corporate Estate Planning 57
Gifting 57

8   The Corporate Fortress; How to Keep It Strong

Corporate Formalities 61
Annual Meetings 63
Bylaws 64
Minutes & Resolutions 64
Keeping at Arm's Length 66

9   Building a Powerful Corporation

Corporate Responsibilities 71
Corporate Formalities Checklist 73
Issuing Stock 75
Types of Stock 76
Bank Accounts 77
Federal Employer Identification Number 78
Corporate Record Book 80
List of Officers, Directors, and Agent of Form 81
Funding Your Corporation 81

10   Finding a Nevada Home

Resident Agent 83
NCH 84
Reputation 85

11   Total Taxation

Paying and Filing Income Taxes 87
Tax Deductions 91
Selected Business Expenses 91
Tax Chart of Some of the Taxes Levied in Each of the 50 States 98
Corporation Organization and Entrance Fees Initial Taxes 106
Federal Tax Charts 112
Federal Estate Tax 113

12   "Nevada for Under $350"

Step by Step, How to Incorporate in Nevada 116
Sample Articles, Bylaws, Minutes and Resolution 117

13   Glossary of Terms 141

14   Useful Websites 145

ACKNOWLEDGMENTS

I wish to thank the entire staff at Nevada Corporate Headquarters, Inc. for their support and assistance throughout the writing of this publication. They have continued to support my work and all of the varied and diverse clients that come to them for assistance in setting up Nevada corporations.

Also, I thank my wife, Jennifer, my son, Luke, and my daughter, Lian, for their love and encouragement during the long hours spent on this book. Much of my life's joy and pleasure comes from them and it is through their strength that I continue to challenge myself in new ways.

Additionally I would like to send my thanks and admiration to my friends and family whose relationships I will always hold close to my heart. There are many unnamed parties who have lifted me to new heights and to whom I will always remain dedicated and I thank them all.

Most importantly, I give thanks to God, who provides direction and guidance as we move along our journey through this beautiful experience of life.

INTRODUCTION

Today's world of high taxes, economic uncertainties, booming litigation and privacy innovation have caused an overwhelming interest in Nevada Corporations. American families and businesses are coming to Nevada, through incorporation, to stabilize their financial situations. Nevada corporations have already helped tens of thousands of Americans gain an edge on the next century even as present uncertainties are at an unprecedented high. The benefits of incorporating in the Silver State are just now becoming widely known.

Nevada adopted its Revised Statutes for Corporations in 1987. Its creation was based primarily on Delaware corporate statutes, which have attracted businesses from around the nation for the past century. Nevada, a long-time pro-business state, was looking for new ways to increase its revenuers without having to tax its citizens or businesses. Sales, gaming and room taxes have always been the main sources of revenue for the state. As Nevada continued to grow, however, new ways of obtaining revenue were sought. The idea of attracting revenue to the state by providing businesses with very favorable incorporating conditions proved to be a successful new source of revenue for the state and a new vehicle for the entrepreneur. As a result, the State of Nevada now collects approximately $30 million annually form corporate fees.

Nevada's corporate laws are attracting people from around the country who are looking for an edge. Nevada made its process for incorporating simple, inexpensive and painless. Delaware and Nevada are comparable because they both have quite favorable corporate statutes. However, Nevada looked at Delaware's statutes and took them one step further. They allow complete anonymity for the owners of corporations. Consequently, to maintain privacy, the only choice is Nevada.

Nevada has struck to its guns in remaining a "no tax state" on behalf of its citizens and businesses, which is an additional significant attraction to incorporate in Nevada, whether you live in our out of the state. Any income earned by a Nevada corporation will not be taxed one cent by the State of Nevada. All Nevada requires is its annual state fee, which is minimal, compared with the cost of doing business in states, live New York and California.

Nevada embodies the western free spirit. Gambling and gun-slinging are part of its culture. In general, Nevadans are independent people and believe that government should be kept small and out of people's lives as much as possible. The corporate culture created by Nevada embodies that credo. A Nevada corporation is given the same respect and status that each and every citizen of Nevada is given. Unlike those of many other states, Nevada's courts are sticking behind their corporations to protect the rights of representatives to remain separate from and corporate liability. Many statutes this country are now allowing lawsuits to "pierce the corporate veil", making the officers and directors personally responsible for the debts and actions of a corporation. Nevada law clearly makes the actions of a corporation's representatives exempt from personal responsibility, except in cases of outright fraud. This should be reason enough for the business persons to consider Nevada as their place of incorporation, because no matter what you are operating, a lawsuit must be directed at the place of legal origin in order to sue corporate representatives personally.

Nevada corporations also attract people from around the country who are interested in protecting their personal assets and keeping their private lives as a private as possible. Personal assets such as real estate, cash and securities can be held in a corporation, out of the reach of anyone attempting to take them from you.

With all this in mind, let's get incorporated! The objective of this guide is to give you the necessary to begin to incorporate in Nevada. By doing it yourself you can save money and, better yet, give yourself the opportunity to see and understand the entire incorporation process instead of having an attorney do it for you. This way, you can be sure of what has taken place without spending a lot of money to get there! Also, it is empowering to realize your own potential and ability to create a corporate entity. All too often, we are left with the belief that some task or hurdle in front of us cannot be overcome-yet with effort, we can create the world we want to live in. It all commences with the effort to expand your knowledge and your abilities each and every day.

I have created this guide to incorporate in Nevada with simplicity in mind, including the emphasis on essential information that you will need to get your corporation off on the right foot. I have made arrangements with a resident agent whom I recommend for your use, Nevada Corporate Headquarters, Inc., located in Las Vegas, the commercial center of Nevada. In exchange for promoting their services, they have agreed to answer your questions and help you get properly set up and started. Therefore, as you move through this guide, I encourage you to call them at 1-800-398-1077 to clear up any questions that may arise.

If you purchased this book with the intention of doing it yourself, but have decided that you still would prefer to have someone else get your corporation set up and operating, I recommend that you use Nevada Corporate Headquarters, Inc. They provide the lowest cost, highest level, most complete range of services. For your benefit, I have asked Nevada Corporate Headquarters to introduce themselves and their services in the final chapter of this guide.

CHAPTER 1
THE PERILS OF BUSINESS

The scene is all too familiar: After college, Rich realizes there's no happiness or money to be made by reporting to someone else everyday. He starts to consider the future security of his new family. He decides to venture out on his own and fulfill that dream that has been yanking at him for so long. Not too sure about how he should go about structuring his business, Rich risks missing many details that would later lead to his financial demise. He couldn't foresee the lawsuit that would threaten everything he had worked for, including the nest egg he had put away for his young daughter's college education.

Everyday, countless lawsuits are filed against small businesses, while at the same time; the risk of tax hikes for entrepreneurs becomes greater. These are the two major reasons entrepreneurs should be concerned about learning the appropriate way to structure their businesses.

Usually, entrepreneurs who are looking for the easiest way to structure their businesses will choose a sole-proprietorship or a partnership entity. What these individuals fail to realize is the long-term implications of starting their businesses without proper structuring. They have started the business as an individual and will be responsible as an individual.

Every entrepreneur should start any business venture as a corporation. If the business venture fails, the corporation will allow them to protect their personal assets and carry any losses over to the next business venture. Have you ever met an entrepreneur with just one business idea?

The other concern many experienced entrepreneurs have is deciding in which state they should establish corporations. For years, Delaware was the first choice. Today Nevada has taken the lead. Today's world of high taxes, economic uncertainties, booming litigation and privacy invasion has caused an overwhelming interest in Nevada corporations. American families and businesses are coming to Nevada, through incorporating, to stabilize and protect their financial situations. Nevada corporations have already helped hundreds of thousands of Americans gain an edge on the next century even as present uncertainties are at an unprecedented high. The benefits of incorporating in the Silver State are just now becoming widely known.

LITIGATION

In today's litigious world you can easily find yourself in a financial crisis that could cost you most, or all of your assets. Each year, thousands of families are suddenly wiped-out. Don't think for a minute it couldn't happen to you! Nearly 50,000 new litigation cases are filed each week.

No matter how safe and secure you feel today, you can never be certain that your lifetime accumulation of wealth won't suddenly disappear tomorrow. There are too many ways to get into financial trouble today. We are all vulnerable. Tomorrow you can be unexpectedly hit with:

- A lawsuit by business partners
- A professional malpractice lawsuit
- A major damage suit for injury around your home or business
- A tax audit and a large IRS assessment
- A costly uninsured motor vehicle accident
- Unanticipated medical bills
- A divorce
- A suit for defamation of character

The above examples are very real. Consider the alarming statistics below:

- There's a 50 percent chance you will someday divorce.
- 2,000,000 businesses will start up this year. In six months 500,000 will fail; in one year another 1,000,000 will fail.
- If you have been in business under five years, there's an 85 percent chance you will fail. What liabilities will you have? What assets do you plan on losing (the new car you bought for your son that is still in your name)? What asset do you least want to lose (the savings you've put away for you and your spouse's retirement)?
- Statistically, businesse owners have a one in four chance of being involved in a lawsuit.

• Statistically, you have a one in ten chance of being hit with one or more devastating lawsuits in the next ten years.

TAXES

What about tax problems? Roughly 4 million Americans are audited each year, and many taxpayers are faced with tax bills they can't afford to pay. The IRS has armed enforcement officers that will raid individual's businesses and homes to collect on past due taxes. As a sole proprietor, the risk of dealing with the IRS is 10 times greater than as a small corporation.

Then you have to deal with the state tax agencies, such as the California Franchise Tax Board. The Los Angeles Times dated August 2, 1999 stated that "State Agency rivals the IRS in toughness...Franchise tax board is ruthless, arrogant, unwilling to compromise."

Thanks to Nevada's three main industries — gaming, tourism, and mining, Nevada is one of only four states with no corporate income tax. Nevada has no franchise tax, no taxes on corporate shares, and no succession tax. Every corporation formed in the United States, however, is subject to federal income taxes. Corporate federal tax is lower than personal income taxes in most every case, which is another reason to consider incorporating before you proceed in your business venture.

CHAPTER 2
WHICH BUSINESS STRUCTURE IS RIGHT FOR YOU?

ENTITY COMPARISON CHART

Type	Liability Protection	Tax Savings	Privacy	Simple To Form	Low Cost
Sole Proprietorship	None	None	None	Yes	Yes
General Partnership	None	None	None	No	Yes
Limited Partnership	LP - Yes GP - None	None	Possible	No	No
Limited Liability Company	Yes	Possible	Possible	No	Can Be
Corporation	Yes	Yes	Yes	Can Be	Can Be

SOLE PROPRIETORSHIPS

The sole proprietorship is the least expensive form of business to establish, however, other factors may make it become the most expensive entity in the long run.

There is no legal distinction between yourself and the sole proprietorship. Any business liabilities are also your personal liabilities. If you are sued, you may receive a judgment against your personal assets. Your sole proprietorship cannot survive you, meaning your ownership interest ends when you die.

There are no formalities to maintain, no meetings to hold, and no documents to draft and file. Although there are no formation hoops to jump through to set up the proprietorship, its business activity must still fall within federal, state, and local guidelines.

From a tax standpoint, as a sole proprietor, you do not have to file a separate business tax return. A Schedule C is attached to your 1040 and filed with the IRS. Taxes are paid on whatever personal income tax applies to you. Gains and losses from the business are simply combined with other personal taxable items.

Since there are no differences between business and personal assets, the sole proprietor risks everything they have in the business. If a judgment is awarded against the business, every personal asset of the owner can be used to satisfy the judgment. Additionally, a sole proprietorship can find it difficult to raise capital, since it can only be accomplished if the individual can qualify for a personal loan.

Sole proprietorships have been historically limited in their ability to participate in such things as federally qualified pension plans and medical reimbursement plans that are available to other business entities. They may have trouble justifying full deductions for certain business expenses.

From an estate-planning standpoint, sole proprietorships have several basic planning considerations that are particular to proprietorship status. If the proprietor wants to pass the business to his or her heirs, there are a number of estate planning and taxation issues that must be overcome.

All in all, the sole proprietorship is certainly not a long-term business solution. If you are currently a proprietor, you are not only gambling that you will not incur business liability, but you are ignoring the many tax advantages available to you.

Sole proprietorships may be easy to maintain and are often recommend by accountants and attorneys. However, there are many issues to consider that these professionals often forget or ignore. The way the world works today, it would be foolish to just assume that you are immune to losing your assets and that your privacy won't be invaded. The United States is one of the most litigious societies in the world. We live in a place where someone who chooses to visit your home, invited or not, can sue you if he or she trips on a buckled rug. We live in a society where if you spill a cup of coffee on yourself, you can get millions out of the company that sold you the coffee. Think about it. Do you really think you're safe?

With approximately 800,000 attorneys in the U.S. today looking to survive, businesses new and old must take precautions to protect their interests. Sole proprietorships are risky entities that could cost you and your family all you own, especially understanding that there is no other entity more scrutinized by the IRS.

ADVANTAGES

Ease of Formation: A sole proprietorship only requires a business license and DBA (doing business as) to be filed in your city or county and you're in business.

Pass-Through Tax Treatment: The income, profits, losses and expenses of the company flow directly through to the individual who reports the income and expenses on his/her personal tax return.

DISADVANTAGES

Personal Liability: The individual is responsible for all the debts and obligations of the business and creditors can lien personal property even if it's not part of the business.

Lack of Continuity: If you die or are sick, the business dies or languishes.

Lack of Investment Flexibility: Sole proprietorships are usually financed through capital contributions of the individual, or by debt.

GENERAL PARTNERSHIPS

Rich decides that he could use some help in opening up his business, Widget World. He decides to call up his college buddy, Guy, who was always good with finances. After all, he was their fraternity's treasurer and bookkeeper, so Rich and Guy form a partnership.

This type of entity is formed when two or more people come together for the purpose of conducting a business. As Rich and Guy decide to form their partnership, they must agree on which duties they will each take on and what percentage of ownership they will each hold. Typically this is done with a partnership agreement that should be put together by a lawyer.

Similar to sole proprietorships, partnerships have many of the same advantages and disadvantages. Like sole proprietorships, partnerships are easy to form, but are taxed according to the tax levels of each partner. Likewise, no liability protection is offered either. Again, businesses should seriously consider the consequences of litigation without any shield to protect individuals' personal assets.

ADVANTAGES

Ease of Formation: A general partnership is a voluntary association of two or more individuals or business entities who agree to work together for a common business purpose. They share their profits and losses equally, or as otherwise stated in an agreement.

Pass-Through Tax Treatment: By forming a partnership, Rich and Guy's profits and losses from the business are recorded on their personal income tax returns.

DISADVANTAGES

Personal Liability: Rich and Guy are each personally responsible for all the debts and obligations of the business. If one partner makes a mistake, it may cost both partners.

Lack of Continuity: If one of the partners ceased to be a partner, whether by retirement or by death, the partnership is usually dissolved as a matter of law.

Lack of Investment Flexibility: General partnerships are usually financed through capital contributions of the partners, or by debt. They can only use limited partners to raise money for the partnership without giving up management responsibility.

LIMITED PARTNERSHIPS

Limited partnerships are composed of a minimum of two types of participants: general partners and limited partners. General partners accept the responsibility for and take all risks involved in managing and conducting the business. Limited partners, on the other hand, are investors who share some risk, depending on the amount invested, but have no participation in the actual management of the entity. Limited partners simply enjoy the profits and losses stipulated in the partnership agreement. These provisions provide limited liability protection, but they do not allow any privacy for the parties involved.

Limited partnerships are often used for estate planning purposes. These vehicles allow individuals to control their assets, while still having the ability to pass ownership of those assets along to their heirs. Limited partners can substantially minimize taxes on estates worth over $600,000 ($1.2 million for couples). Estate planning requires careful preparation often involving other entities as well. Be sure to consult tax-planning experts before considering this option.

ADVANTAGES

Pass-Through Tax Treatment: The income and losses of the business flow through to the individual partners in accordance with their partnership shares.

Financial Flexibility: A limited partnership can take on more limited partners to raise additional capital.

Charging Order: If a person with interest in a limited partnership is involved in a lawsuit for any reason and loses, the judge/jury may award damages to the other party. If this happens the person will have to disclose their interest in the limited partnership. This can be assessed to satisfy the judgment by means of a judgment lien. However, most attorneys will not have their clients take this kind of lien because of the disadvantages to their client. The general partner controls the distribution of profits that come out of the limited partnership. If the general partner sees that a creditor has taken ownership of the interest of the limited partnership they can decide not to distribute profits yet still send a K-1 distribution reporting to the IRS that states the creditor is responsible for the tax obligation of the distribution that never happened.

Discounting: Family Limited Partnerships take advantage of the discounting allowed by the IRS. Discounting occurs when the heirs of an estate who have interest as limited partners take over the estate due to a death. The heirs can take the value of the limited partnership and discount the value by as much as one third. This will lower any estate taxes due.

DISADVANTAGES

Liability of the General Partner(s): The general partner is fully liable for the obligations of the business. Many general partners will insulate themselves through incorporation.

Lack of Control for the Limited Partners: The limited partners are legally precluded from participating in the management of the business. If limited partners do exercise management or control they can lose their limited liability protection and have personal exposure of the obligations of the business.

Lack of Investment Flexibility: General partnerships are usually financed through capital contributions of the partners, or by debt. They can only use limited partners to raise money for the partnership without giving up management responsibility.

LIMITED LIABILITY COMPANIES

Limited Liability Companies have been around for many years in such countries as South America and Germany, but first came to America in 1977 in Wyoming.

Evidence of LLC legislation in other states around the country did not take place until the IRS made a key ruling on the taxation of this new structure. On September 19, 1998, the IRS issued Revenue Ruling 88-76, stating that LLC's would be taxed as partnerships even though none of the members (partners) or managers would be personally liable for any of the company's debt. This ruling encouraged other states to adopt this new vehicle as well. All states have accepted LLCs into their domain as legitimate business structures.

The LLC structure can be used to hold property and transact any type of business. LLC structures are similar to partnerships, limited partnerships, "S" corporations, and trusts. An

LLC is a flow-through entity. It passes all of the LLC profits and losses directly to the members of the LLC. Individual members are therefore taxed at their personal tax rates.

Nevada statutes only require one individual or legal entity to form an LLC. However the IRS has the ability to tax the LLC with only one member as a corporation or a partnership. In most cases, the need to set up an LLC is driven by the need to take advantage of the partnership pass-through income. In that case you would need to have two persons or legal entities as members. Some view this requirement as a disadvantage because of control issues, but there are alternative strategies to abate those concerns. If used creatively, this rule can be used quite effectively. A combination of an LLC and other entities is required, but it could include you and your corporation, you and your trust, or two corporations. In essence, you can be your own partner. If used properly in conjunction with corporations, privacy can be maintained as well.

LLCs can also be handy tools when exploring joint ventures. For example, let's say you are enjoying the benefits of controlling your own corporation and you now want to combine efforts with another individual by forming a joint venture. Taking two corporations that you control and forming an LLC will allow the profits or losses from the joint venture to flow directly into your respective corporations. The taxable entity in this case would be the corporation. This is a simple way to bring two corporate entities together and keep at arms length from the business at hand.

LLC TERMINOLOGY

LLCs Are Owned by Members: They are like shareholders in a corporation. Unlike "S" corporations, which are limited to 35 shareholders, the LLC can have an unlimited amount of members. Some states even allow one member to own the LLC. The jury is still out as how this will be taxed by the IRS. It is best to stick with two-member LLCs.

Membership Interest: A member's ownership interest in the LLC is referred to as a "membership interest." It is like stock in a corporation.

Articles of Organization: *Articles of Organization* are like the *Articles of Incorporation* of a corporation and *Certificate of Limited Partnership*; they are filed with the state. They usually include:

- The name of the LLC
- The county where its principal place of business is to be located
- The date the LLC will be dissolved if the business is not perpetual (Nevada allows for perpetual LLCs, most states do not)
- The appointment of an agent for service of process

Some states also require you to list whether it is managed by members or by managers. In Nevada you must list either the manager's name or two members' names.

Generally, their members, who vote in proposition to their ownership interests, manage LLCs. If the LLC is to be managed by one or more managers, the articles of organization should include a provision to that effect.

Operating Agreement: The operating agreement establishes the rules for the operations of the LLC business. It is similar to the bylaws of the corporation and the partnership agreement of the partnership. The operating agreement controls things such as profit and loss and how management powers are divided up with members or managers. It is recommended to have an operating agreement because it is always smoother to have decisions like distribution of profits put in writing before the LLC gets started. Unless the operating agreement says otherwise, the operating agreement can only be amended with the written consent of all members.

Organization Documents: This refers generally to either the LLC's articles of organization or operating agreement, or both.

Manager: All members of an LLC can manage the business; it can be delegated to fewer than all members, or to a single manager. A manager can be an individual, a partnership, and a corporation or in some states, such as Nevada, even another LLC. Managers may appoint officers, but aren't required to do this. The Articles of Organization would specify the scope of the manager's authority, if any.

Default Provision: If the members do not specify their business relationship with each other in the operating agreement, the rules in the state apply by default. Provisions imposed on the members are known as "default provisions." In some states, members deem certain default provisions so important that they can't be changed even by agreement. These are known as "bulletproof provisions," or the acts known as "bulletproof acts."

WHAT ARE THE DISADVANTAGES OF AN LLC?

Lack of Uniform LLC Law: The Conference of Commissioners on Uniform State Laws is now drafting a *Uniform Limited Liability Company Act*. However, things are still unclear about taxation and state laws are determining these rules.

Federal Security Limitations: The LLC is only available to privately owned companies. If a company were to go public, it would have to be a "C" corporation. With *merger laws* it would be relatively easy to convert an LLC to a "C" corporation.

Loss of Pass-Through Tax Treatment: This would occur when an LLC would be viewed as a corporation. This happens when there is an election filed with the IRS and the LLC qualifies for three of the four criteria that define what a corporation is. If it is taxed as a partnership this is not true.

State Tax Treatment: Some states impose an income or franchise tax on the LLCs.

CHAPTER 3
CORPORATIONS ... WHICH ONE?

One of the most consistently dynamic business structures is the corporation. Offering tremendous flexibility and advantages that generally outweigh all other business structures, the corporation is the most secure entity in business. In the next chapter, you will see the many benefits of incorporating. This chapter will compare various types of corporations.

GENERALLY UNDERSTOOD DEFINITION

Black's Law Dictionary defines a corporation as:

> An artificial person or legal entity created by or under the authority of the laws of a state or nation, composed, in some rare instances, of a single person and his successors, being incumbents of a particular office, but ordinarily consisting of an association of numerous individuals, who subsist as a body politic under a special denomination, which is regarded in law as having a personality and existence distinct from that of its several members, and which is by the same authority, vested with the capacity of continuous succession, irrespective of changes in its membership, either in perpetuity or for limited term of years, and of acting as a unit or single individual in matters relating to the common purpose of the association, within the scope of the powers and authorities conferred upon such bodies by law. A franchise possessed by one or more individuals, who subsist as a body politic, under a special denomination, and are vested by the policy of the law with the capacity of perpetual succession, and of acting in several respects, however numerous the association may be, as a single individual.

BUSINESSES TAXED AS A CORPORATION

The rules you must use to determine whether a business is taxed as a corporation changed for businesses formed after 1996.

Business formed before 1997. A business formed before 1997 and taxed as a corporation under the old rules will generally continue to be taxed as a corporation.

Business formed after 1996. The following businesses formed after 1996 are taxed as corporations.

1. A business formed under a federal or state law that refers to it as a corporation, body corporate, or body politic.

2. A business formed under a state law that refers to it as a joint-stock company or joint-stock association.

3. An insurance company.

4. Certain banks.

5. A business wholly owned by a state or local government.

6. A business specifically required to be taxed as a corporation by the Internal Revenue Code (for example, certain publicly traded partnerships).

7. Certain foreign businesses.

8. Any other business that elects to be taxed as a corporation by filing Form 8832.

CORPORATIONS

Although a corporation is separate and distinct from its stockholders, directors or officers, it is a separate entity that can act only through its members, officers, or agents and cannot have knowledge or belief of any subject independent of the knowledge or belief of its people. A stockholder (owner or partial owner) is a holder of shares of stock in the corporation and is NOT IN LEGAL DANGER for the acts of the corporation. In other words, you, as the owner, are not responsible. A stockholder is not the employer of those working for the corporation nor is he the owner of a corporate property.

A corporation is a citizen in the state wherein it was created and does not cease to be a citizen of its state of domicile by engaging in business or acquiring property in another state. Since corporations are solely creatures of Statute, their powers are derived from the constitution and laws of the state in which it is incorporated. As an artificial person, a corporation is considered to have its domicile in the state where it is incorporated and the place where it has a statutory presence. When the corporation functions in a different state, the site of its designated resident or registered agent is sometimes called its "statutory domicile".

The existence of the corporation is not affected by the death or bankruptcy of a shareholder, officer, or director. It has a continuous existence as long as it complies with the statutory requirements of the state where it is incorporated.

Once brought to life, this artificial entity has most of the rights and privileges that a person has. A corporation can own and operate businesses, hire employees, buy and sell goods and services, make contracts, rent office space, have checking and savings accounts, maintain retirement plans for employees, and can sue and be sued.

Although the corporation is a legal "person" with rights of its own, a corporation cannot walk, talk, think, or act for it self. It cannot market its products, nor can it perform any of the physical tasks required to operate a business. You and those hired to work within the structure of the corporation do all of this.

The important point to remember is that when you own a corporation, the corporation exists as a separate entity or person. You can live anywhere you choose, in any state or country, but it is the corporation that conforms to the requirements of the state in which it resides. You will find that Nevada is the State with the greatest benefits to protect you and your corporation.

"C" VERSUS "S"

Corporations vary in their structure and organization. A corporation is not just a corporation. You will need to select from various types. The two typical corporations that most CPAs or attorneys will recommend are "S" and "C" corporations. In explaining the differences between the "S" and "C" corporation, one should keep in mind that every state has different laws for corporations. What an accountant may tell someone in California may not be true in Nevada.

The "C" corporation allows for limited liability of the owners, officers, and directors. The "C" corporation will run it's accounting on a fiscal year rather than a calendar year. This allows the "C" corporation to determine which month it's year-end for filing taxes will be. All profits of a "C" corporation are taxed at the corporate tax rates and reported on a separate tax return from an individual, which is called the 1120. Profits of the corporation can be left in the corporation as retained earnings, as long as the amount does not exceed $250,000. However, you can have more than $250,000 if you can show that the corporation needs the money for future growth.

The "S" Corporation also allows for limited liability of the owners/officers/directors. However the "S" corporation will typically run on a calendar year and the biggest difference is that all profits of the corporation pass through to the individual owners personal 1140 tax return. There are no tax brackets separate from the personal tax brackets for an "S" corporation as there is for a "C" corporation.

There are several other differences between the two types of corporations, which we will show by describing the "S" corporation in detail.

"S" CORPORATIONS

There are certain qualifications that the corporation must meet in order to elect S-corporation status. To elect S-corporation status your corporation must meet all the following requirements:

1. It must be a domestic corporation formed in the USA.

2. It may have no more than 75 shareholders.

3. It may only have individuals, estates or certain trusts as shareholders.

4. It may not have nonresident alien shareholders.

5. It may only have one class of stock.

6. It must be a small business corporation (financial institutions such as banks, insurance companies, building and loan associations or mutual savings and loan association cannot take advantage of electing S-corporation.

7. It must conform to state statutory restrictions, which limit the transfer of shares/ownership, of the company.

An S-corporation operates on a December 31st calendar year ending. However, as with most rules there are exceptions. The corporation can make a Section 444 election, which generally allows for a tax year ending September 30, October 31, or November 30, but estimated tax payments must be made that would offset any advantage a shareholder might gain by having an offsetting fiscal year.

CONSIDERATIONS WHEN ELECTING AN "S" CORPORATION

1. When losses flow through the corporation, those losses can be used to offset ACTIVE income from either spouse (active income includes income derived directly from business activity).

2. If the "S" corporation earns ACTIVE PROFITS they can be offset by losses from other businesses and or operating expenses from a sole proprietorship.

3. There is no double taxation.

4. There are no penalties for excessive accumulated earnings for "S" corporations.

5. The "S" corporation shareholder / employee may only deduct 25% of the cost of medical insurance as adjustment to income.

6. The "S" corporation must report paid premiums for health premiums and group term life insurance as taxable income if the shareholder owns more than 2% of the stock.

"C" CORPORATIONS

Every *Fortune 500* company is a "C" corporation. "C" corporations have different tax rates than individuals. In almost every category, "C" corporations will pay less in tax than an individual. The "C" corporation tax table is unique from the personal tax rates, because as you start making millions your tax rate drops. "C" corporations have no limitations on shareholders. Shareholders can live anywhere in the world and can be any type of entity. "C" corporations will give you the most flexibility and are recommended by this author in most instances.

The only thing you will have to be concerned with when using a "C" corporation is double taxation. "S" corporations allow the profits and losses of a corporation to flow directly through to the owners/stockholders of the corporation. All of this takes place without taxation at the corporate level. This eliminates the potential for double taxation. Double taxation of a "C" corporation occurs when the corporation has its profits taxed initially, and then the dividends paid out to shareholders are taxed again on the personal level.

Eliminating or deferring profits through proper financial management can easily deal with this problem. Double taxation typically only occurs with large corporations who have several stockholders that need the profits distributed to them at the year-end of the corporation. The owner of a corporation can decide at the end of the year what to do with the profits. They can distribute them to the owners in the form of a dividend (not recommended), pay bonuses (wages), which are tax deductible to the corporation, keep retained earnings or have a retirement plan that profits are distributed to on a tax deferral basis. Retained earnings can be used for future growth in the company, additional investments in equipment, buying another company, advertising expenses, etc. When the corporation has retained earnings, these profits are taxed at the corporate level, left in the corporation and not distributed to the owners. If the corporation's owner or officers need the money for personal expenses, pay a wage to the owner in the form of a year-end bonus, or expense as much from the corporation as possible by having a retirement plan set up. The IRS says that it is the taxpayer's responsibility to lower their tax liability. They also say that a corporation can deduct any general related business expense, by using good money management.

Another key factor in deciding which type of corporation to use is personal privacy. Every corporation that elects "S" status will be letting the IRS and the state tax authority know who the owners of the corporation are. Since all profits and losses flow through to the owners, there is no privacy in this structure. If you are incorporated in Nevada and set up a "C" Corporation, ownership is completely hidden, as Nevada is the only state that does not require the owners to be listed on any state records.

PRIVATE VS. PUBLIC CORPORATIONS

A public entity is registered with the SEC (Securities Exchange Commission) and has stock available for purchase on one of the stock exchanges. A private corporation is one in which the ownership of the company is not available for sale on any market.

CLOSELY HELD CORPORATIONS

A family or close group usually owns a closely held corporation and shares are not to be sold outside the family or group. A corporation is a closely held corporation if at any time during the last half of the tax year, more than 50% in value of its outstanding stock is owned directly or indirectly by or for five or fewer individuals.

For the passive activity rules, a corporation is closely held if all of the following apply.

1. It is not an "S" corporation.

2. It is not a personal service corporation.

3. At any time during the last half of the tax year, more than 50% of the value of its outstanding stock is directly or indirectly owned by five or fewer individuals. "Individual" includes certain trusts and private foundations.

To figure if more than 50% in value of the stock is owned by five or fewer individuals, apply the following rules.

1. Stock owned directly or indirectly by or for a corporation, partnership, estate, or trust is considered owned proportionately by its shareholders, partners, or beneficiaries.

2. An individual is considered to own the stock owned directly or indirectly by or for his or her family. Family includes only brothers and sisters (including half brothers and half sisters), a spouse, ancestors, and lineal descendants.

3. If a person holds an option to buy stock, he or she is considered to be the owner of that stock.

4. When applying rule (1) or (2), stock considered owned by a person under rule (1) or (3) is treated as actually owned by that person. Stock considered owned by an individual under rule (2) is not treated as owned by the individual for again applying rule (2) to consider another the owner of that stock.

5. Stock that may be considered owned by an individual under either rule (2) or (3) is considered owned by the individual under rule (3).

DOMESTIC CORPORATIONS

A corporation operated in the state in which it was formed.

FOREIGN CORPORATIONS

A corporation that is doing business in a state other than that in which it was formed.

ALIEN CORPORATIONS

A corporation formed in a country other than where it is doing business.

NONPROFIT CORPORATIONS

A nonprofit corporation is one recognized by the IRS as tax-exempt, and is organized for a public or charitable purpose. A nonprofit corporation must have at least five directors or trustees, and upon dissolution must either distribute its assets to the state or federal government, or another entity.

The American Cancer Society and the Muscular Dystrophy Association are two notable entities organized as nonprofit corporations, and many cities in the U.S. are host to many local nonprofit corporations organized to meet local needs. For private purposes, however, the nonprofit has severe limitations.

Most corporations that are formed "for-profit" are allowed to engage in "any lawful business activity". Nonprofit corporations are required to state a specific purpose that benefits either the public at large, a segment of the community, or a particular membership-based group.

Contributions to 501(c)(3) corporations are exempt from federal or state taxation. Many wealthy individuals make substantial contributions in their estate plans for qualified nonprofit corporations. These estate plan contributions are actively pursued by many nonprofits as part of their campaign for public support.

For tax purposes, the nonprofit corporation must be formed for religious, charitable, scientific, educational or literary purposes in order to claim 501(C)(3) tax-exempt status.

ADVANTAGES:

- No taxes paid on income
- Lower postal rates on third-class bulk mailings
- Less expensive advertising rates
- Eligibility for many state and/or federal grants
- Nonprofits are exclusive beneficiaries of free radio and television Public Service Announcements (PSAs) provided by media outlets

501(C)(3) ELIGIBILITY RULES:

- Organized and operated for charitable, educational, religious, literary or scientific purposes
- Not distribute gains to directors, officers or members
- Distribute any assets remaining upon dissolution to another qualified tax-exempt entity or group

- Not participate in political campaigns for or against candidates for public office

- Not substantially engage in grassroots legislative or political activities except as permitted under federal tax rules

PERSONAL HOLDING CORPORATIONS

The Internal Revenue Service designates any corporation with over 60 percent passive income, whose stock is owned (more than 50%) by not more than five people at any time during the last half of the tax year, as a "personal holding company". To determine the stock ownership requirement, the rules consider stock owned by a corporation, partnership, or estate to be owned proportionately by its shareholders, partners, or beneficiaries. Because of high tax rates, you want to avoid having your corporation classified as a personal holding corporation.

Income to a personal holding company is taxed at personal income tax rates, instead of corporate income tax rates, as long as it is being distributed. If it is not distributed, a surtax of 39.6% on undistributed earnings is applied. Personal holding company income includes the following:

- Taxable income from estates and trusts

- Payments under personal service contracts

- Dividends, interest, royalties, and annuities, including royalties from mineral, oil, gas, and copyrights

- Rent adjusted for the use of, or the right to use corporate property, with certain exceptions

PERSONAL SERVICE CORPORATIONS

Personal Service Corporation is another label you want to avoid. There is a 35% flat tax on all personal service corporation profits. Personal service corporations are generally owned and operated by lawyers, accountants, and consultants. There are two tests to qualify for this status. The first is a functional test; the second, an ownership test. Just let those creative juices start flowing as you read this.

For this purpose, a corporation is a personal service corporation if it meets all of the following requirements.

1. It is not an "S" corporation.

2. Its principal activity during the "testing period" is performing personal services. The testing period for any tax year is the previous tax year. If the corporation has just been formed, the testing period begins on the first day of its tax year and ends on the earlier of:

    a. The last day of its tax year, or

b. The last day of the calendar year in which its tax year begins.

3. Its employee-owners substantially perform the services in (2). This requirement is met if more than 20% of the corporation's compensation cost for its activities of performing personal services during the testing period is for personal services performed by employee-owners.

4. Its employee-owners own more than 10% of the fair market value of its outstanding stock on the last day of the testing period.

Personal services are those in the fields of accounting, actuarial science, architecture, consulting, engineering, health (including veterinary services), law, and performing arts.

A person is an employee-owner of a personal service corporation if both of the following apply.

1. He or she is an employee of the corporation, or performs personal services for or on behalf of the corporation (even if he or she is an independent contractor for other purposes), on any day of the testing period.

2. He or she owns any stock in the corporation at any time during the testing period.

One way to avoid personal service corporation status is to sell something. Sell a law book instead of consulting others on the law. Sell product, give seminars or do something that is more tangible. The other simple way is to forfeit ownership over the corporation. Sell part of the corporation to non-employees. If you have a corporation and you have income coming in, yet you are not an employee (but maybe a contractor for that corporation), then your corporation will not be labeled as a personal service corporation.

Plan your relationship to the corporation carefully. Find at least one reliable person who can help you by owning a percentage of the entity in case you need to distance yourself from the corporation. In-laws are a good example of people to use with your corporate strategy because they are not your immediate family. Always have somebody around to help you out if you need to move ownership quickly out of your own name.

HOLDING CORPORATIONS

A holding corporation is different than a personal holding company. The holding corporation status is when one corporation controls other corporations, usually called subsidiaries. A corporation maintains control of a subsidiary when it owns at least 80% of its stock. The IRS will allow or may request a holding corporation to combine their income and expenses and file a consolidated tax return. Banks will also accept a consolidated financial statement when applying for credit lines.

CHAPTER 4
CORPORATIONS STILL #1

WHY INCORPORATE?

Many people think that because they are a single person or a family, rather than a business, that incorporating is not for them. Wrong! Incorporating can offer your business many advantages! A corporation is a legal entity created separately from those who own and operate it. As a separate entity, the corporation's debts and taxes are separate from its owners (shareholders), thereby, offering the greatest personal liability protection of all business structures. Because the corporation continues to exist even after the death of a shareholder, it offers tremendous estate planning advantages. In addition to liability protection, incorporating offers attractive tax advantages, prestige, the road to better financing and the ability to raise cash. Corporations can also be used to own real estate, automobiles, yachts, or aircraft while providing health and life insurance, retirement benefits and expense accounts.

Every business owner needs to protect his/her personal and business assets from litigation. Last year more than $27.7 billion was awarded to employees of U.S. businesses. In 1999 the largest award ever by a jury to victims of a car crash, was over $5 billion dollars, to be paid by a U.S. company.

INDIVIDUAL VS. CORPORATION

One of the major reasons individuals incorporate is the fact that, as individuals, we earn money, pay taxes, and buy things, but a corporation earns money, buys things, and *then* pays taxes. What would you rather do, pay for things with pre-tax or after-tax dollars?

The following illustration shows how one individual, who has $60,000 per year in revenue, can save him almost $10,000 in taxes just by incorporating. The power of being able to determine what you pay yourself, and what stays in the corporation for future expenses of the company, is what draws millions of people to incorporating rather than running their business as a sole proprietor or partnership. The illustration does not take into account several areas that would make the illustration more compelling, such as retirement accounts and fringe benefits. Additionally, this example does not include state taxes, which can be anywhere from 4% to 12%.

Independant Contractor
John Doe

Revenues	$60,000
Expenses	$10,000
Gross Profit	$50,000
Income Tax	$11,042
Self-Emp. Tax	$ 7,650
Total Taxes Paid	$18,692
Total Net	$31,308

Corporate Plan
John Doe, Inc.

Revenues	$60,000
Expenses (includes 1/2 FICA)	$11,530
Salaries Paid	$20,000
Gross Profit	$28,470
Corporate Tax	$ 4,270
Net Profit	$24,200
John's Income	$20,000
John's Income Tax	$ 3,000
Total Taxes Paid	$ 8,800
Total Net	$41,200

LIABILITY PROTECTION

- Over 94% of all lawsuits are filed in the U.S.

- Over 40 million lawsuits are filed each year in the U.S.

- 90% of all lawyers worldwide live in the U.S.

- Chances of being involved in a lawsuit are one in four next year

While most small businesses know that incorporating can shield personal assets in the event of a frivolous lawsuit, many are lulled into complacency by an "it-won't-happen-to-me" attitude. This thinking has resulted in tremendous losses to many unprepared business owners. No other structure gives you and your business the liability protection offered by a corporation. In such a litigious society incorporating makes good sense.

Nearly every state has adopted statutes that limit the liability of corporate representatives including officers, directors, and shareholders. Nevada has gone a step further with specific statutes stating all corporate representatives are free from personal liability resulting from corporate activities, except in the case of fraud.

Corporations can be sued, file bankruptcy, and be involved in other unfortunate activities and never jeopardize the personal assets of corporate agents or representatives. The Nevada "corporate veil" has never been pierced except for instances of outright fraud!

Corporations as business structures provide liability protection to everyone involved with the business. From the investor or stockholder to the officers, corporate liability stops with the corporation. Any activity that a corporation gets into that is not fraudulent in nature will not adversely affect the personal life of any of the corporation's participants.

Unlike a sole proprietorship or even a partnership, a corporation can accumulate debt without ever making its officers, directors or stockholders responsible for the repayment of that debt. If a corporation gets itself into a lawsuit, the outcome of that lawsuit can affect the corporation directly, but the participants cannot be held responsible.

Corporations are used in the business world today primarily for liability protection. Corporations came into existence to limit the direct responsibility of all participants for the faults or debts of a business. An individual can invest money in a corporation and that investor's potential loss will be limited to the amount of money invested and no more.

Because of the obvious advantages of limiting the amount of personal liability that one takes on by operating through a corporation, many strategies have been developed to protect the assets of businesses that have potential lawsuit risk. In addition, other strategies have been developed to protect the assets of individuals because of our crazy and litigious society.

ASSET PROTECTION

It doesn't take a catastrophic lawsuit to wipe out everything you own. There are many common business events that can equally affect small businesses, leaving the owner's personal assets fully exposed. For example:

- One or more of your largest customers could stop paying their bills or file for bankruptcy

- New technologies, competition, new legislation or market conditions could render your product or service obsolete or significantly reduce the demand

- You could suddenly become incapacitated and unable to manage the operations of the business

Could you satisfy all business obligations, without tapping into personal reserves or losing personal assets? Existing assets (bank accounts, homes, cars, etc.) are not the only targets for creditors. Unrealized assets such as future earnings, inheritance, and insurance settlements are also at risk in the event of an unfavorable judgment.

TAX SAVINGS

The myriad tax benefits that can be achieved by utilizing a corporation outweigh those available through the use of any other business structure. Many of the tax benefits available to a corporation can greatly benefit corporate owners. Since President Clinton's 1994 personal income tax increases were initiated, corporations have had a lower federal tax rate at all levels of income compared to individual rates. There has never been a better time to own a corporation.

Nevada's popularity is based on the fact that the state does not tax its corporations. Unlike most states in this country, Nevada has taken a "pro-business" stance. Nevada's legislatures have consistently recognized that taxing business is the wrong approach to maintaining a healthy state economy. Which delivers more dollars—increasing sales, reducing costs, or cutting taxes?

It may surprise you to learn that, from a pure cash-in-your-pocket point of view a tax dollar saved is much more valuable to you than an added sales dollar or a cost savings dollar.

A tax dollar saved is a full dollar retained in the business. The federal and state governments take a tax bite out of every other business dollar—whether it's a dollar that was retained by reducing costs or a dollar that was brought in by increasing company sales. If you still aren't convinced of the critical importance of paying close and constant attention to possible tax savings, here's the proof:

TAX SAVINGS VS. INCREASING SALES

$$\frac{\text{Tax Savings}}{(100\% - \%\ \text{Tax Rate})\ \text{times}\ \%\ \text{Profit Margin}} = \text{Sales Equivalent}$$

For example, XYZ, Inc. operating at a 10% pretax profit margin (pretax profits divided by sales) and in an overall 35% tax bracket (federal and state), did some comprehensive tax planning with its advisers and saved $10,000 in taxes. That tax savings is equivalent to the profit on $153,846 in additional sales, computed as follows:

$$\frac{\$10,000}{(100\% - 35\%)\ \text{times}\ 10\%} = \$153,846$$

Thus the $10,000 tax savings brought XYZ, Inc. the after tax profit equivalent of almost $154,000 in additional sales; each $1,000 of tax savings equaled $15,400 in increased sales.

TAX SAVINGS VS. CUTTING COSTS

Assuming an overall tax of 35% on your company's taxable income:

Pretax Margin On Sales	Saving $1,000 in Taxes	Saving $1,000 in Costs
20%	$7,692	$5,000
15%	$10,256	$6,667
10%	$15,385	$10,000
8%	$19,231	$12,500
4%	$38,462	$25,000

As shown above, if you have a 10% profit margin, a $1,000 savings in taxes is equivalent to $15,385 in sales and a $1,000 reduction in costs is equivalent to $10,000. This is a difference of $5,385 just for spending time on tax savings strategies rather than cost cutting measures.

RAISING CAPITAL

For the person looking to raise capital for a business or project, the corporate structure is superior to all others. Corporations allow investors an opportunity to participate in the profitability and growth of a business without having to participate in its day-to-day activities. Through the sale of stock to investors, a corporation is able to raise capital at all phases of its life cycle. This process can be kept simple by limiting the number of investors. If a corporation is planning to raise large amounts of capital, however, or wishes to solicit more than twenty-five potential investors, the rules and regulations are quite stringent.

These are the primary reasons that many individuals and businesses decide to incorporate. There are also many secondary reasons that just may make all the difference for you. Some of those reasons are:

- Control and management of a corporation is very structured and clearly understood.

- Losses by smaller corporations can be deducted personally.

- Real estate can be controlled within a corporation for the ultimate in asset protection.

- Corporations never die—they have a potentially perpetual existence.

- A corporation can provide you with free health care.

- Many personal expenses can be paid by a corporation, including your car, education, legal and accounting fees, insurance, moving expenses, seminars, books, meals, entertainment, travel, computers, office equipment, and much more.

- Ownership can be easily transferred between generations.

- Corporate pension plans can allow you to put a lot of tax-deferred money away for retirement.

The list goes on and on!

Reducing Audit Risk

The minute you incorporate your audit risk is dramatically reduced. The IRS targets sole proprietorships and general partnerships, while leaving small corporations alone. The IRS sees an individual operating as a sole proprietor or those as a general partnership to be less sophisticated. The IRS also assumes that because they are operating as one of these two ways, they are more likely to cheat on their return. According to the IRS, operating your business as a corporation means you have a higher sophistication level and are less likely to cheat on your taxes.

Corporations can be targets for the IRS, even if small closely held corporations are not. Corporations targeted by the IRS are those with assets over $250,000 or revenue over $3,000,000. These large corporations are seen as a big money maker for the IRS. If a corporation with $25,000,000 in profit is off on their taxes just by a small percentage there is a large tax collection that could still be made. The IRS will spend time with those companies that feel they will get the most from.

Living the Corporate Lifestyle

As an officer or owner of a corporation, you should take advantage of living the corporate life. Why pay for your automobiles, travel, computers, office equipment, certain utilities and even your kid's college education with after tax dollars? A corporation can be structured in ways that allow these expenses to benefit the officers and owners.

Sports arenas rely on corporations to pay for the VIP boxes to watch their sporting events. Corporate owners love to take their clients and employees to these events and they do all of it with pre-tax dollars. Join the country club with a corporate membership and golf every day with no "out of pocket" expense. With these "perks," you will find you don't need to be paid as much salary and will have a lower personal tax liability as well. Get started today, living the corporate life.

BUILDING CREDIT

You can build credit with a new corporation without using your personal credit history. Just as an individual can apply for credit, so can a corporation. A new corporation seeking credit is similar to a young adult applying for credit for the first time. It may take some persistence in obtaining the credit lines wanted, but it can be achieved. NCH, Inc. has credit builder packages available to assist you with the information necessary to start the process in establishing corporate credit. See the website **www.creditandcommerce.net** for a more detailed description of how to build credit with your corporation.

ESTATE PLANNING

One of the most practical uses of a corporation is in providing for a convenient transfer of wealth and assets to one's heirs. The corporation allows for assets that would otherwise be difficult to split up evenly because of their very nature, to be divided and controlled in precise increments.

Your corporation can be a helpful intermediary for disposing of property. Under this plan you would transfer selected assets to your newly organized corporation in exchange for its shares of stock. You can then bequeath or transfer to your designated beneficiaries the desired amount of shares. These shares may be distributed either all at once, or over a period of years, to take advantage of the annual gift tax exclusions. The advantages are:

- Property held in the corporation may be safer from creditors than if owned by the donor or recipient of donations.

- The donor gains considerable flexibility in selecting the number of beneficiaries as well as the division of ownership each will receive.

- Property can be gifted immediately through shares, while it may not be feasible to divide or split the assets.

CORPORATE IMAGE

Image is vital in business today! The words "Inc.," "Incorporated," and "Corporation" command respect and promote a professional image. Individuals and businesses visualize incorporated companies on a higher level than sole-proprietors or partnerships. Major lending sources and credit card companies look more favorably upon corporations. Projecting the corporate identity allows the owners and their personal assets to remain private and separated from the day-to-day operations of the business.

The IRS even believes that incorporated businesses have a higher degree of sophistication. The IRS audits 8.4% of all sole-proprietors and only .76% of corporations with net profits lower than $1 million. They know that corporations are less lucrative to audit, allowed more deductions and taxed at a lower rate.   Very successful corporations often keep attorneys and CPAs on staff to combat the likelihood of an IRS audit.

CORPORATE ADVANTAGE

Take advantage of the favorable tax laws and friendly business structures afforded Nevada corporations like Intuit", Amazon.com", Purchase Pro", Porsche", Home Shopping Network". Even major movie stars such as Madonna have incorporated in Nevada.

Incorporate today and put your business in the same league as the Fortune 500! Incorporating gives any sole-proprietor or small business the benefits that major corporations have always enjoyed.   Limited liability, tax savings and asset protection are just a few of the benefits incorporating can afford smaller businesses.

CHAPTER 5
THE CORPORATION HAVEN: NEVADA

HISTORY OF NEVADA CORPORATIONS

Nevada adopted its Revised Statutes for Corporations in 1987. Its creation was based primarily on Delaware corporate statutes, which have attracted businesses from around the nation for the past century. Nevada, a long-time pro-business state, was looking for new ways to increase its revenues without having to tax its citizens or its state businesses. Sales, gaming, and room taxes have always been the main sources of revenue for the state. As Nevada continued to grow, however, new ways of obtaining revenue were sought. The idea of attracting revenue to the state by providing businesses with very favorable incorporating conditions proved to be a successful new source of revenue for the state and a new vehicle for the entrepreneur.

In recent years, an increasing number of business organizations have filed in Nevada. The number of new corporations filed annually rose 75% between 1994 and 1999. Nevada in 1999 became the ninth ranked state in the nation in the number of new corporations filed—that doesn't even include Limited Liability Companies and Limited Partnerships. Even with Nevada's approximate population of only 2 million in the entire state, nearly 60,000 businesses were filed in 2000. As soon as all the figures are in that should move Nevada into the top five states with the most corporate filings. The top states are those with the highest population, such as California, New York, Texas and Florida.

So, what's the big difference between Nevada law and the laws of other states? The laws of Nevada provide for the protection of corporate officers and directors in specific ways, as opposed to protecting at-large shareholders. For example, under NRS 78.7502, a corporation for any action may indemnify officers and directors whether, "…civil, criminal, administrative, or investigative…." If they are a, "…director, officer, employee or agent…" (Etc.) "…against expenses, including attorney's fees, judgments, fines and amounts paid in settlement…" Similarly, under NRS 78.752, "A corporation may purchase and maintain insurance or make other financial arrangements on behalf of any person who is or was a director, officer, employee or agent of the corporation, or is or was serving at the request of the corporation as a director, officer, employee or agent of another corporation, partnership, joint venture, trust, or other enterprise for any liability asserted against him, and liability and expenses incurred by him, in his capacity as a director, officer, employee or agent, or arising out of his status as such, whether or not the corporation has the authority to indemnify him against such liability and expenses." Furthermore, except in the instance of the commission of fraud by a corporate principle, the decision by a Board of Directors to indemnify a principal is final and may not be set aside judicially. This kind of protection is afforded to Nevada corporate principals even in the face of their having been negligent in the performance of their duties as corporate officers and directors. It is these types of things that attest to the determination of the Legislature of Nevada to continue along a course that is favorable to the tradition of protection of corporate principals in Nevada.

Another significant way in which Nevada's statutes protect corporate principals lies more in what they DO NOT require, rather than in what they do require. Specifically, in many states, normal annual corporate filings require the inclusion of significant financial information about both the corporation as well as its principals. In Nevada, filing requirements are minimal. Nevada states that it does not have an information sharing agreement with the Internal Revenue Service, which is true. However, what really protects Nevada corporations in this area is the fact that Nevada really only has very limited information to share with anyone, the IRS included. In other words, by not requiring anything more than minimal filing information, Nevada does not have anything but minimal information to share. And frankly, with a subpoena from a court of proper jurisdiction, any investigative agency or attorney could access any files held by a state agency as a matter of executing the court's power. Minimal filing requirements cannot be overlooked to contributing to a powerful corporate haven. It is really a rather simple solution to one of the most potentially invasive aspects of corporate ownership.

Another attractive aspect of Nevada corporate law is the tremendous flexibility afforded to corporate principals, especially directors, in controlling the operations and functions of the corporation. So, in addition to specific protection through indemnification, there is also great flexibility in determining just how much control the directors will have in directing the business of the corporation. This is accomplished through statutory allowances made for the primacy of what is stated in the articles of incorporation or the bylaws of a corporation in determining how a corporation will function. These allowances are stated so as to give these primary documents greater direct authority than even the statutes, over that specific corporation, so long as these issues are directly addressed in the by-laws or articles and are not contrary to public policy.

This is in direct contrast to many other states whose laws set out specific guidelines and limitations for director actions, in many areas of corporate activity, such as voting, and the formalization of corporate decisions. This degree of autonomy that directors and shareholders are imbued with in Nevada makes direct control of the corporation much more subject to the desires and intentions of those principals than in many other states.

WHAT NEVADA CASE LAW SAYS

A review of Nevada case law also reveals that while corporations have existed in Nevada since before it was even admitted as a state to the Union, it wasn't until the 1950's that Nevada's Supreme Court began to seriously consider setting aside the corporate veil as a means of compensating someone that had been damaged by the acts of a corporation's principals. (See **Nevada Tax Commission v. Hicks**, 73 Nev. 115, 310 P.2d 852 (2957)). Even so, Nevada courts have traditionally been unwilling to pierce the corporate veil except in those various instances in which a fraud has been perpetrated to the damage of another, and circumstances are particularly egregious. Since 1978, a Nevada court has actually pierced the corporate veil only one time, and that was in 1987. (See, **Polaris Industries Corp v. Kaplan**, **103 Nev. 598, 747 P.2d 884 (1987) and Mosa v. Wilson-Bates Furniture Co.**, 94 Nev. 521, 583 P.2d 453 (1978))

From 1957 to the present, a consistent theme that has run through each of the cases in which Nevada courts have been willing to set aside the corporation's shield and find a principal liable for the corporation's actions has been the perpetration of a fraud by a corporate principal, that has damaged another party. What is significant about this general rule, is that while the courts have heard cases in which corporations have been accused of many things, including responsibility for personal injuries, the failure to maintain corporate formalities, breaches of contract, not having issued stock, failing to select officers and directors, or even having meetings, none of these things in and of themselves have caused a Nevada court to set aside the corporate veil. On the other hand, courts in other states have consistently pierced corporate veils for no more than any one of the infractions listed above. The essential difference being that in other states it has been the intention of their legislatures to assertively protect the interests of non-principal, at-large shareholders.

In contrast, it has always been the intention of the Nevada legislature, since it first sat session in 1864, to allow businesses to operate freely, and with the assurance that so long as they were not breaking the law to the detriment or harm of another party, they could rely on the protections afforded corporate principals by that form of business entity. It is interesting to note that in 1983, the Nevada Supreme Court determined NOT to pierce a corporate veil in a case in which the defendant corporation was capitalized with a mere $1,100.00 (but was entering into contracts worth tens of thousands of dollars), had no directors or shareholders, had held no organizational meetings of any kind, kept no formal minutes or records of corporate transactions, and did not even have a corporate minute book in which to keep corporate records (See, <u>Rowland v. LePire</u>, 99 Nev. 308, 662 P.2d 1332 (1983)). What the Court did find however, was that because the corporation DID have a contractor's license, (which allowed it to legally contract to perform such services), it had a checking account not commingled with those of its principals, and it transacted business with the State's Employment Security Division, that the corporation was not a sham or merely the alter ego of the principals.

Even with these cases, it is not recommended to ignore corporate record keeping. The need to maintain corporate records goes beyond the possibility of having the corporate veil pierced. Such instances where someone will want to look at the records of the corporation are: audit by a tax agency, investors looking into the viability of the corporation, or a principal needing to see the history of how the company has dealt with specific situations in the past.

14 FACTS THAT MAKE A NEVADA CORPORATION'S SHIELD ULTRA STRONG

1. There has never been a case in which a Nevada corporation has been pierced, whenthe corporation has been properly run.

2. Nevada courts have pierced a corporate veil only one time in the last 21 years, and that was because of fraud resulting in harm to another party.

3. Nevada courts have developed a strong record of case law, which protects the corporate veil, making it one of the most difficult in the country to pierce.

4. Nevada is the only state that can indemnify a corporate principal and protect their privacy. Officers and directors are required to list only their name in public records.

5. Nevada requires that only a corporation's president, secretary, treasurer, and one director be listed on the Initial List of Officers, as well as the annual list to renew the corporation's filings with the state.

6. Nevada's indemnification laws vary from those of other states in that they can limit the personal liability of corporate principals, without that officer or director having to prevail in a lawsuit as a defendant, before the corporation is allowed to indemnify him or her. Most states follow Delaware in requiring an officer or director to prevail in a lawsuit before the corporation is even allowed to indemnify that person.

7. Nevada requires only minimal disclosure of personal information at the time of start-up and at the time of annual filings. This ensures the privacy of individuals.

8. Nevada is the only state, which does not share information with the Internal Revenue Service by means of a formal agreement.

9. Nevada does not require the filing of an amended list of officers or directors if new officers or directors are elected or appointed after filing and during the year.

10. A Nevada corporation may be formed for the express purpose of limiting a person's liability in a lawful business venture.

11. Unlike many states, and as an added dimension to the indemnification of corporate principals, Nevada law allows for the establishment of alternate financial arrangements to protect corporate officers and directors. These include but are not limited to the creation of a trust fund for such eventuality, self-insurance, securing the obligation through the granting of a lien on corporate assets, or placing a letter of credit, surety or guarantee, to be drawn on in time of need. The value of this is in giving the corporation additional resources to draw upon to protect its officers and directors in the event of a lawsuit.

12. Nevada law allows for the most minimal capitalization of a corporation, thereby removing this as a means of piercing a corporation's protective shield. Capitalization can be done with tangible or intangible property, including services to be rendered to the corporation in the future.

13. Nevada requires NO statutory minimum capitalization at the time of start-up.

14. Through broad empowerment allowances, Nevada law specifically provides for a corporation's principals to be given control over such things as the establishment of stock privileges, voting rights, the issuance of shares, etc. through provisions in the articles. These infuse the directors with tremendous flexibility and control over the affairs of the corporation since major changes in policy and procedure can be accomplished through an amendment of the articles rather than relying solely on the statutes.

COMPARISON OF STATE STATUTES BETWEEN NEVADA AND OTHER SELECT, KEY INCORPORATION STATES

	Nevada	New York	California	Texas	Delaware
State laws allow for piercing the corporate veil	Yes	Yes	Yes	Yes	Yes
Courts regularly uphold piercing statutes	No	Yes	Yes	Yes	Yes
State laws provide for the privacy of corporate officers and directors	Yes	No	No	No	No
Statues provide for the permissible indemnification of officers and directors	Yes	No	No	No	No
State laws provide for minimal capitalization of corporations	Yes	No	No	No	No
State laws provide for ease of incorporation through minimal filing requirements	Yes	No	No	No	No

PIERCING THE CORPORATE VEIL

One more reason Nevada ranks above other states when it comes to privacy is because of its policies regarding accountability. Unlike other states, Nevada believes that the individuals controlling corporations should not be in jeopardy of losing their personal assets because of corporate matters; and likewise, corporations should not be responsible for the personal liabilities of its controllers.

California, for example, views corporate structuring quite differently than Nevada. Whereas "C" Corporations separate the individuals controlling corporations from the entities themselves by definition, California courts often make people responsible for corporate misfortunes.

Clearly opposite from Nevada's rationale, more times than not, California courts will "pierce the corporate veil" making the individuals vulnerable and scrutinizing people for corporate matters. This means that an officer's personal assets could be attacked leaving his/her home, savings, and assets completely at risk. So, the main advantage Nevada has over other states can be summed up in just one word—PRIVACY.

To illustrate just how important incorporating in Nevada really is, consider the following information about piercing the corporate veil in Nevada as opposed to other states. Nevada, offering personal and financial privacy, makes it extremely difficult to pierce the corporate veil. The court case that follows shows the value in Nevada statutes.

ROWLAND VS. LEPIRE

In 1983, the Supreme Court of Nevada rejected an attempt to pierce the corporate veil in **Rowland vs. Lepire** (99 NV 308, 6621 2nd at 1337). The defendant failed to maintain any corporate documentation, neglected to have any formal meetings for directors and shareholders, and drove the net worth of the corporation into negative numbers. No dividends were paid out to shareholders. No officers received salaries. No corporate record book even existed. Despite all the evidence against him, the court ruled that, "Although the evidence does show that the corporation was undercapitalized and that there was little existence separate and apart from (the two key shareholders) . . . the evidence was insufficient to support a finding that appellants were the alter ego of the corporation." In this case the evidence was considered insufficient to prove that the individuals were the "alter ego" of the corporation meaning that the officers would be considered the same as the corporation.

Fortunately, Nevada has a stringent three-prong test to prove that one is an alter ego of the corporation. The burden of proof rests entirely upon the plaintiff(s). All three parts to the test must be proven in order to pierce the corporate veil; failure to prove any one part will result in failure to pierce the veil. Two of the most difficult points to prove are "fraud" and " intent of fraud." With a nearly insurmountable task in front of them, lawyers often abandon efforts before they have even begun.

HOW NEVADA IS BECOMING #1 IN INCORPORATION SERVICES

FINANCIAL PRIVACY

Nevada has developed a corporate structure unlike that of any other state. Previously the preferred state in which to incorporate was Delaware. Nevada created their corporate statutes based on those of Delaware and then improved upon them. Nevada statutes allow investors and owners of Nevada corporations to remain completely private. Most states in this country require that you publicly file the name and address of a corporation's directors, officers, and stockholders. This information can then be publicly accessed by a brief telephone call to the

Secretary of State's office in the state of incorporation. Nevada, in an attempt to create a private corporate shelter, requires only the name of the corporation's president, secretary, treasurer and the corporation's directors, specifically excluding vice-presidents and stockholders. The state does not wish to know who the investors or stockholders of the corporation are.

A Nevada corporation owner can utilize the privacy of contracted officers and directors for his corporation. Consequently, they are the only visible public representatives of their corporation. The owner can still hold the corporate title of vice-president, remaining completely in control, but out of the public's eye. This makes Nevada the preferred state of incorporation.

NO IRS RECIPROCITY

Nevada takes corporate privacy very seriously. The Secretary of State's office (which is responsible for corporations) does not ask for detailed information and therefore does not have much information to share. Even the former Governor of Nevada took a public stand on refusing to submit to the Internal Revenue Services' requests for a program of information sharing.

In 1992, the Internal Revenue Service came to then Nevada Governor Bob Miller requesting that he establish an information exchange program. The IRS wanted Nevada to exchange all of the information they have on every resident and corporation in Nevada, in exchange for a reciprocal arrangement with the IRS database. This type of automatic exchange system is done in most other states in the U.S. The Governor stood his ground and told the IRS he wanted no part of the program. He even brought out the state media to record his bold stand!

Nevada currently does not keep much information on its residents, whether individuals or corporations. An exchange program would have committed Nevada to an information-gathering program. Fortunately, Nevada still remains America's domestic and corporate safe haven.

ASSET PROTECTION OVER OTHER STATES

Almost every state in the United States has adopted corporate statues that limit the liability of corporate representatives, including the officers, directors and stockholders. Nevada has very specifically defined in its statutes all corporate cases where fraud has been perpetrated. This means that the corporation can be sued, file bankruptcy or be involved in other unfortunate activities and still not jeopardize the personal assets of its agents or representatives. The significant thing to remember here is that if your corporation does get sued, the initiator of the suit must bring the action against the corporation in its state of domicile. This is where it becomes important to have set up your corporation in a state that has taken a stand to protect the personal liability of a corporation's participants. Nevada has taken this stand quite firmly. We will take a look at those statutes later.

Today, states like California are allowing lawsuits to penetrate a corporation's veil of protection. Directors and officers of a corporation are being sued personally for the corporation's actions. This recent turn of events is reason enough to make Nevada your corporate base. Nevada's courts have taken a firm stand to prevent lawsuits against a corporation from personally affecting the corporation's representatives.

"TAX-FREE" STATE

Pro-business Nevada, unlike almost every other state in this country, has taken a stand! The state has continued not to tax the income of its corporations or its citizens. Imagine a state that believes taxes should not come directly from the income of its citizens or businesses. This almost sounds like capitalism!

Corporations are entitled by law to many deductions not available to individuals. It's the responsibility of each individual taxpayer to structure his or her business affairs in such a manner as to minimize your tax liability. While tax evasion is a serious crime, legal tax avoidance is the duty of every business owner.

Your Nevada corporation will not be required to pay any other hidden taxes, such as franchise taxes, capital stock taxes or inventory taxes. You may be required to pay sales tax if your Nevada corporation is selling products in Nevada.

LOW COST

Nevada is one of the lowest cost states in which to incorporate. Nevada only charges a filing fee of $85 per year. (Note that these fees are subject to change.) For a mere $85 annually, Nevada will give you the right to all the benefits of a Nevada corporation.

NO MINIMUM CAPITAL REQUIREMENTS

A Nevada corporation can be organized with very little capital if desired. Many states require that a corporation have at least $1,000 in capital.

ONE PERSON REQUIREMENT

One person can hold the offices of president, secretary, treasurer, and be the sole director. Many states require at least three officers and/or directors. Thus, there is no need to bring other persons into a Nevada corporation if the owner does not desire it.

NO NEED TO COME TO NEVADA

A corporation can be formed by mail, fax, or phone and the person incorporating never has to visit the state, even to conduct annual meetings. Meetings can be held anywhere in the world at the option of the director(s).

Chapter 6
Live and Work Anywhere You Want But Incorporating In Nevada is a Must

Anyone Can Own a Nevada Corporation

Anyone in the United States can incorporate their business in any state they choose. By doing so they will be governed under the laws of the state of incorporation, if brought into a court of law. (See previous chapter.) However, if you are incorporated in a specific state and choose to do business in another state you will need to file as a foreign corporation in the new state and be held to the tax code of that state.

To file as a foreign corporation in the state in which you are doing business, you will need to call the Secretary of State's office or visit the web site of that state. Every state has different requirements to file.

How do you know if you need to file in another state as a foreign corporation? As a general rule, if you have a storefront or a license (such as a contractor) in that state you have to file in order to be authorized to do business there. Some businesses such as internet marketing, network marketing or a consulting business operating in several states can set up their base of operation anywhere. For instance, if you are sitting on a beach in Tahiti and have a network marketing business and someone calls you, can you conduct business there? Absolutely. This means no matter where you are you can be making money in your business. The same is true of a website business. This differs from a restaurant located in Seattle, Washington, for example. If the restaurant is not open you don't make money, no matter where you are.

If you are one of the lucky few that can use a Nevada corporation for the tax benefits as well, you will need to set up the business as a real live operation in Nevada. Nevada corporations can be utilized and maintained by individuals who are not residents of Nevada. A person can establish a Nevada corporation without ever having visited Nevada.

Working in conjunction with a competent resident agent can make this process much simpler. Your resident agent should be able to assist you along the way and provide your corporation with the services necessary to allow you to establish a base in Nevada. Your resident agent should be able to save you the expense of traveling to the state to acquire an office for your corporation. By providing you with the use of their facilities and staff, they can complete all necessary corporate work.

A NEVADA BASED CORPORATION

Everyone utilizing a Nevada corporation for tax advantages should base their business in Nevada by having:

1. A Nevada bank account, so that wherever you are located, all corporate funds are maintained in Nevada. This gives credence to the fact that your corporation is truly based in Nevada.

2. Your corporation should utilize a Nevada address for all of its corporate mail. This further legitimizes your Nevada base for anyone that may be looking into your business.

3. The corporation needs to establish a Nevada phone number. This line should be answered with your corporation name, and its name should also be listed in the local phone book.

4. If you need further proof of a Nevada base, it is a good idea to have a business license in the county or city of your resident agent.

All of these legitimizing factors help to prove that your corporation is based in Nevada. It now looks and operates like any other Nevada-based business.

WHAT A NEVADA CORPORATION TAKES WITH IT ACROSS STATE BORDERS

When you are conducting a business in your home state you still have the choice of deciding which state to incorporate in. Although it would be nice to take advantage of the tax benefits of other states rather than your own, you are subject to local and state tax in the state in which you are doing business. So why would you want to incorporate in another state?

Take Nevada law with you! One of the many things that make a corporation such a powerful entity within which to place a business enterprise is that it is durable. Not only in terms of time, but also, given the right protection by the laws of its state of incorporation, it can also weather the storms of litigation. What does this mean for the principals of a Nevada corporation that live in, and do business through that corporation in another state? First, in some very important instances, if that Nevada corporation is sued in another state, and it is properly registered to do business in that state, that state's courts will use NEVADA law to adjudicate certain issues. Second, the obvious advantage to this is that when you incorporate in Nevada, which has powerful laws protecting its corporations, you can take those protections with you across state lines. This dramatically enhances the protection (limitation of liability) that that corporation can give you as a corporate principal.

WHEN WILL NEVADA LAW APPLY OUTSIDE OF ITS OWN BORDERS?

Remember that a Nevada corporation can conduct its internal business according to the laws of Nevada, no matter where its principals decide to live, work, or conduct the internal business of the corporation. This includes matters such as:

- When and where to have corporation meetings
- The issuance of dividends
- Purchase, lease, or acquisition of property by the corporation
- Entering into contracts for and on behalf of the corporation
- Election of officers
- Appointment of Directors

As a general premise, "Choice of Laws" doctrines are widely accepted and understood across the country and require a home state's courts, (home state to the Nevada corporation's principals) in which a "foreign" corporation is registered to do business, to use the foreign corporation's state laws to adjudicate various aspects of a case, if that foreign corporation is sued in a home state. The doctrine of choice of laws is most often augmented through decisions made by the courts, as opposed to specific statutes. But when does it apply?

The Nevada Supreme Court has said that, "…a crucial function of choice-of-law rules is that their application should further harmonious relations between states and facilitate commercial intercourse between them. If we disregard this important conflicts function…we would perhaps rarely find another state's laws controlling. Consequently, the clear intentions of the parties would be defeated." (See, **Sievers v. Diversified Mortgage Investors, 95 Nev. 811, 603 P.2d 270A (1979)**)

CHAPTER 7
CREATIVE CORPORATIONS

PRIVACY STRATEGIES

Privacy is the one feature Nevada offers that no other state in the country can. Aside from tax savings and liability protection, privacy is the number one reason people from all over the world incorporate in Nevada. Nevada is the only state in the country that does not require disclosure of information about corporate ownership, stock, or capital. Individuals are therefore allowed to keep very low profiles about business matters and personal assets. Also remember that although Nevada does want to know the names and addresses for the president, secretary, treasurer and directors of a corporation, they leave the vice presidency open—this is where nominee officer services come into play. Privacy and Nevada corporations go hand in hand. As previously stated, Nevada is one of the only states in this country that does not ask for any information regarding the ownership of their corporations. This allows individuals to keep a very low profile with respect to the business they are involved in and the assets they own.

NOMINEE OFFICER SERVICES

Owners of Nevada corporations who wish to remain out of the spotlight should consider using the nominee officer service available through Nevada Corporate Headquarters, Inc. For a nominal fee, corporate owners can achieve something otherwise unattainable—total privacy and anonymity protection. Choosing the nominee officer service DOES NOT mean that you are surrendering any portion of your corporation or control over it. This process is a simple business transaction wherein you are essentially hiring someone to sign on the public list so you don't have to. The nominee will sign on as all corporate officers (including the president, secretary, treasurer, and director) with the exception of the vice presidency.

Once your name is out of the public eye, you can then manage things from behind the scenes. Remember that the corporate bylaws, nominee officer contract and any other amendment you wish to include, strips the nominee officer of any and all actual power. Keep in mind that contracts protect both parties involved, the owner of the corporation as well as the resident agent providing the service. Liability can run both ways. To lay the rules out in black and white, corporate owners don't want the liability of nominee officer involvement and the nominee officer does not want the liability for the corporation he is signing on for. It is a simple business transaction, a win-win situation.

This system works well because the nominee officer does not want to know anything about the company, and you as the private stockholder have the power to remove their name from the public list at any time. Best of all, you, as the owner, are the ONLY signer on the corporate bank account. Those seeking more privacy than most conventional banks allow might want to consider a brokerage account. Brokerage accounts generally require less personal information; yet still supply convenient banking features.

The owner of a Nevada corporation may hire someone to represent the corporation in the corporate positions that are a matter of public record (president, secretary, treasurer and directors). The owner can then become a vice-president of the corporation to manage and run the corporation. Remember, most corporate bylaws state that in the absence of the president, the vice-president fills in. When you are using a nominee officer as your front representative, he or she most likely will be absent from the day-to-day management of the corporation, and for his or her own sake will not want to know too much about whatever the corporation is involved in. A typical agreement for nominee services will spell out that the only authority of the nominee is to sign the state's list of officers for the corporation. Doing anything more than that would constitute breach of contract.

This system works well because your front officers do not have to know anything about the company. This protects them and lets you, as the private stockholder, remove them at any time. You can take this process one step further and amend your corporate bylaws to strip your president, secretary and treasurer of all their corporate power. This can also be done with a written contract.

One form of nominee service, which leaves control of the corporation in your hands (and your name) for 364 days of the year, involves having the nominee appointed to all positions just prior to the filing of the list of officers and directors with the state. The nominee's name is filed with the state, and immediately after this is accomplished, the nominee resigns, only to be reappointed to all positions of record just prior to the next filing.

TAX SAVINGS

Let's look at creative ways of avoiding (not evading) or reducing taxes. Again, you must remember that all of these strategies have to be properly handled and documented; every piece of paperwork must be in place to ensure that these are planned properly and within the law. Simplified, you are creatively avoiding taxes, which is perfectly legal.

An advantage to working with multiple corporations comes when you look at the tax advantages available for corporations. Corporations are only required to pay 15% in federal taxes, up to $50,000 of profit (considering that there are no additional state taxes such as in Nevada). So, instead of paying a higher tax rate at $150,000 in profits amounting to $37,700, simply set up three corporations which are making $50,000 each, breaking up profits (you don't want to keep all your eggs in one basket) and only pay 15% on the entire amount! There are some considerations that need to be dealt with such as control group issues. A control group is several corporations splitting up income to lower their taxes and all have 51% of ownership with five or fewer shareholders. If you don't have a group of 10-15 unrelated people to distribute ownership to or four unrelated parties that will hold 100% of each corporation, this strategy will not work.

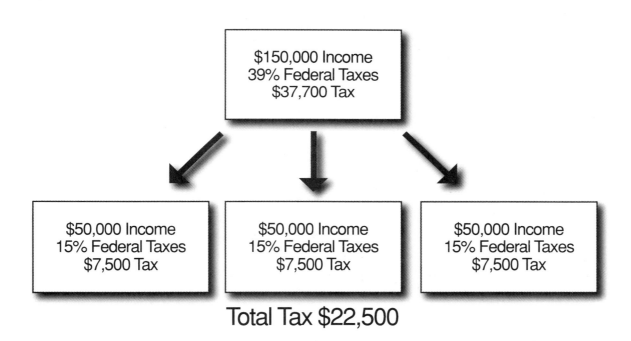

It is best to create a situation where those entities are not just contracting with one another, but with corporations that have real employees. Again, when you create a strategy like this, you want to make sure it is in a state like Nevada where you can keep officers, directors, and stockholders anonymous and create a credible view that they are not all the same entity or individual. As long as there are agreements in place, contracts between these different corporations, and cross billings (not all at once, but in increments) for services rendered or goods produced, validating legitimate transactions will not be a problem. Your paper trail with any of these types of strategies must be clear and complete. If the IRS audits your corporation it is important to have sufficient evidence to support your claims.

HOME STATE CORPORATION STRATEGIES

Nevada is a tax-free state; there are no corporate or personal taxes. This is significant when you compare it to states like California, where you will pay 9.3% on $100,000 or $9,300. By the use of some simple strategies, that $9,300 can remain in your pocket and prepare you for the coming changes that we should be expecting with the new administration.

So how does it work? Unfortunately, everyone will not be able to use these strategies. These strategies work with the self-employed and those who manage their own businesses—small and large. You also need to have unrelated parties who can own the different entities. The first step is to establish a Nevada corporation to work with your current non-Nevada corporation. Then you will want to place the Nevada Corporation in a position where it will be providing a service or leasing equipment or property to your non-Nevada corporation. Your Nevada corporation can act as a supplier, consultant, marketing service, advertising service, management company, or financier. All of these businesses could provide a service to your current home state corporation.

Your current home state business can then divert profits that are being taxed, and direct those profits into Nevada where there will be no state taxes. For instance, if your home state business sells computers, why not have your Nevada corporation purchase the computer from your present supplier, mark it up to near retail, and sell it to your home state business to be resold. You have just left all of the profit from the sale of the computer in tax-free Nevada, and reduced or eliminated any home state tax that you will have to pay. Now, if this strategy is implemented in a high tax state like California, your overall tax savings can be substantial.

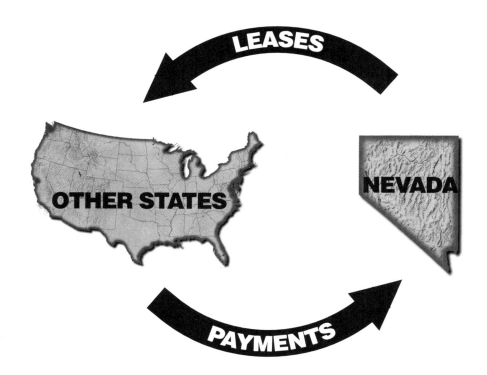

Here's an example: let's say that your California business is doing quite well, and that you are ending up with $100,000 in net profits per year, $9,300 of which is being paid to the state for taxes. Now let's say that you create a Nevada corporation that is going to provide marketing services to your California business. This new business just so happens to charge about $100,000 for the marketing expertise that they are providing your California business. You have now successfully taken all of your profit that would have been left in your California business and taxed for $9,300, and moved it into Nevada. You have just legally saved yourself a bundle.

This same strategy can be modified to fit just about any type of business situation. With businesses going into bankruptcy every day, you need to take aggressive measures for the survival of your business.

FINANCING

When using your Nevada corporation in conjunction with a home state corporation one of the cleanest strategies is to make your Nevada corporation into a financing corporation. In Nevada there is no such thing as usury laws, therefore you can literally charge an interest rate of 25%. If you have the ability to move, let's say $100,000 from a Nevada corporation to your home state corporation as a loan, you can quite nicely draw out $25,000 a year from a state that taxes businesses, to Nevada that does not. You would still pay your federal tax, but you have eliminated all or a substantial portion of your state taxes.

Be sure that with any of these strategies that you utilize that all of your documentation is in place to show that there was resolution to authorize the loan and a promissory note that is signed. You may want to also pledge the assets of your home state business against the note to encumber them.

TAX SAVINGS PLAN

Corporations can act as fantastic tax saving devices for the individual who has left over income at the end of the month. If you are a person who has flexibility over how you receive your income, you may find this strategy useful. It is often best to expense as much of a corporation's income out as possible to avoid profit gain and higher tax rates. Reduction of corporate income is handled through legitimate business expenses. By eliminating any corporate income tax (and also the corporation's exposure). If, however, one of the only ways that you have of eliminating your corporation profits is to draw out those profits as personal income, then you may consider leaving the profits in the corporation.

In working out corporate strategies one needs to look at corporate and individual tax rates. On corporate profits up to $50,000 a corporation pays only 15% tax, unlike personal income tax rates, where on that same $50,000 you would be paying 25% tax, and that is just federal tax. Comparing these rates, it should become clear that if an individual can operate under a corporate shelter and only draw out of that corporation enough income to get by, you would see a 54% savings in tax dollars by leaving money in a corporation and not taking it out.

How can you receive the benefits of those funds now held by your corporation? Well, these unused profits can go towards investments, future business uses, and many other alternatives that would directly and indirectly benefit the corporation's owners. Always remember, though, that once these retained earnings (retained profits) are removed from the corporation as personal income, they would be taxed at your current personal tax rates. However, if you control the corporation, there are many alternatives to taking funds out as personal income, in the form of a salary or dividend.

One option, with the low taxed retained earnings in the corporation, would be to give you an interest free loan. A Nevada corporation can make a loan to one of its corporate officers with no interest attached, and the officer would not need to consider these funds as income. This strategy is a good way for you to personally have the use of corporate funds without paying any personal income tax on funds.

Let's consider another alternative to using these low-taxed, retained earnings or corporate profits for your personal gain without personal tax. In this example, corporate profits (which up to $50,000 are only taxed as 15%) have built up and now amount to a cash accumulation of $150,000. You live in a house approximately worth $150,000. As a corporate officer, you decide to purchase the house as an investment for the business perhaps. As the owner of the property, the corporation would pay you $150,000. You still control your property, but you have just successfully moved $150,000 into your pocket—tax-free! This example does have other implications, but for purposes of this section, we will keep things as simple as possible.

The proper way to balance this strategy is to receive income from your corporation of an amount up to $21,450, which is currently taxed at 15%, and leave the rest of your corporate income in your corporation in the form of corporate profits. You would now have essentially made $71,450 and only paid 15% on the entire amount. (This is not taking into consideration employee or self-employment taxes.)

JUDGMENT PROOFING YOURSELF AND THE CORPORATION

Judgment proofing your corporation means protecting assets within the corporate structure. Judgment proofing can protect either the corporation or you. The strategies can involve multiple corporations or just one. In today's world, lawsuits destroy businesses and lives everyday. As the number of emerging lawyers exceeds demand, litigation situations will become more intense. To limit your exposure and protect your assets is no longer optional; it is a necessity.

One of the main reasons business owners choose to incorporate is to avoid liability that his/her business activities would otherwise expose their personal assets to. Within the corporate structure, personal assets are separated from the liability of the corporation and likewise, corporate assets are protected from personal problems.

Despite the effectiveness of the corporate vehicle, attorneys do not cease to attack. In fact, corporations are increasing targets for lawsuits today. Attorneys assume that corporations have assets and are therefore worthy of pursuit. Today, "just cause" is no longer a prerequisite to engage in litigation. Judgment proofing your corporation is one way to prepare for the future.

One technique used by corporations large and small, is to separate those areas of their business that have a higher likelihood of drawing lawsuits (particularly those branches that work directly with the public), and separating those areas from the more valuable assets under their control. For example, construction companies may consider placing their expensive vehicles and equipment in a separate corporation altogether so that if the main company is sued, not all valuable assets will be attacked. In this case, you might want to set up a leasing corporation to hold the most valuable assets and simply lease the equipment to the construction corporation. Therefore, if someone were to win a suit against the main construction company, the equipment would not be attached to the asset pool enabling owners to simply hand over the main (vacant) corporation instead of fighting senseless litigation.

Another useful strategy for judgment proofing your corporation involves encumbering your corporation with heavy debt. The idea of this strategy is to turn your corporation into a turnip so that anyone considering a suit will find nothing to go after. To initiate the strategy, the corporation you wish to protect borrows money from you personally or from another corporation. The objective is to bury the corporation in debt so that it is unattractive to those seeking to penetrate it. A series of loans can place the corporation at least $100,000 into debt. To secure these debts, the loan benefactors must sign a security agreement with the borrowing corporations. A security agreement is a powerful tool commonly used to secure certain assets as collateral on a loan. Security agreements solidify the agreement between the benefactor and recipient by stating that the assets, receivables, inventory, and everything belonging to your corporation, is collateral for the loans.

Once the assets are secured, file the agreement for public access. The entity that has now secured your property for a loan would file a UCC-1 financing statement with the Secretary of State's office of the state where your corporation is incorporated, and with the county recorder in the county of the assets. This UCC-1 states to the public that these assets are collateral for a note that is owed and that the assets are encumbered. It tells the public that they cannot touch these assets until the debt is paid. Public documentation of encumbered assets alone will sometimes discourage money-hungry lawyers during their initial asset searches. After the UCC-1 agreements are discovered, the attorney, who is no longer smiling, calls his clients back and tells them there is nothing to go after should a suit ensue, but if they wish to continue he will be glad to for an unreasonable retainer. Mission complete. You have now successfully judgment proofed your corporation.

This strategy can be very successful by using a Nevada corporation in conjunction with your home state corporation. Your Nevada corporation would be the lending entity to your home state business that fully encumbers the assets of your home state business. This would allow you as an individual, to remain out of this loop completely because no one has to know that you are the owner of this lending corporation in Nevada.

SECURITY AGREEMENTS

Security agreements are used to secure a loan with the assets of the borrower; for instance, a house, car, or even gold. If you were making a loan to a friend and you wanted to secure it with something that they had, this would be the way of doing it. Then after this was accomplished, you would want to take the next step and file a UCC-1 against the individual. A UCC-1 is a public document that goes on record in the county and/or the state of the borrowing party. The UCC-1 establishes a public record that a particular individual or corporation's assets (maybe a house, a car or something else) are put up for security on a note. You can also add specific clauses in your security agreement that can tie up a business' future value. This agreement is between two parties to encumber an asset or to show that something was put up for a note. The UCC-1 becomes a public document when it is filed.

Every state has its own form of UCC-1 documents. These forms can generally be found at an office supply store or purchased through the state's Secretary of State office. UCC-1's are generally filed at the county level. A UCC-1 is a public notice that validates the encumbering of assets. At the top of the form, the names of the debtors and their addresses and their tax ID numbers are listed boldly. "Area number 4" is where the names of the secured parties would go. Again these are both corporations and their tax ID numbers. "Area number 6," is probably the most significant area because this is where you state exactly what you want the public to know about any kind of arrangement that you have with the benefactor. You would put the amount of the note and what kind of property the note encumbers. It can be a piece of property, a business, or anything of considerable value. The debtor does not have to sign this as long as the creditor has. After it is filed with the county or the state, a filed copy is then forwarded to the secure party.

Filing the UCC-1 from one business against another for non-payment is a way to encumber the assets of a corporation. If you were to use this strategy against another corporation you have a significant interest in, it could keep potential creditors away. However, you use a strategy such as the one below, you should have varying ownership in both corporations.

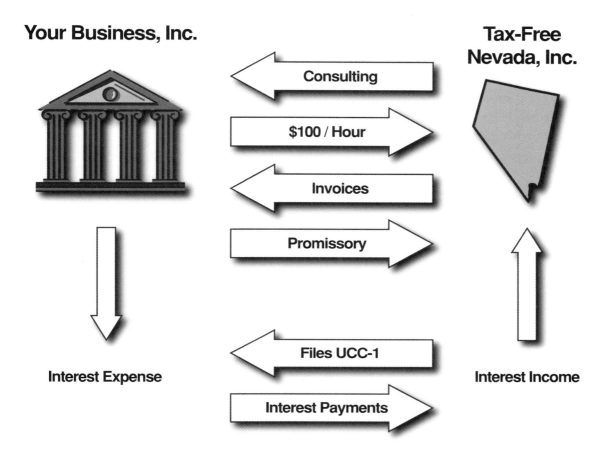

Your Business, Inc.

Tax-Free Nevada, Inc.

Consulting

$100 / Hour

Invoices

Promissory

Files UCC-1

Interest Payments

Interest Expense

Interest Income

NONTAXABLE EXCHANGE OF PROPERTY FOR STOCK

If you transfer property (or money and property) to a corporation in exchange for stock in that corporation (other than nonqualified preferred stock, described later), and immediately afterwards you are in control of the corporation, the exchange is usually not taxable. This rule applies both to individuals and to groups who transfer property to a corporation. It also applies whether the corporation is being formed or is already operating. It does not apply in the following situations.

- The corporation is an investment company

- You transfer the property in a bankruptcy or similar proceeding in exchange for stock used to pay creditors

- The stock is received in exchange for the corporation's debt (other than a security) or for interest on the corporation's debt (including a security) that accrued while you held the debt

Both the corporation and any person involved in a nontaxable exchange of property for stock must attach to their income tax returns a complete statement of all facts pertinent to the exchange.

Control of a corporation. For this purpose, to be in control of a corporation, you or your group of transferors must own, immediately after the exchange, at least 80% of the total combined voting power of all classes of stock entitled to vote and at least 80% of the outstanding shares of each class of nonvoting stock of the corporation.

Example 1. You and Bill Jones buy property for $100,000. You both organize a corporation when the property has a fair market value of $300,000. You transfer the property to the corporation for all its authorized capital stock, which has a par value of $300,000. No gain is included in income by you, Bill, or the corporation.

Example 2. You and Bill transfer the property with a basis of $100,000 to a corporation in exchange for stock with a fair market value of $300,000. This represents only 75% of each class of stock of the corporation. The other 25% was already issued to someone else. You and Bill recognize a taxable gain of $200,000 on the transaction.

Services rendered. The term *property* does not include services rendered or to be rendered to the issuing corporation. The value of stock received for services is income to the recipient.

Example. You transfer property worth $35,000 and render services valued at $3,000 to a corporation in exchange for stock valued at $38,000. Right after the exchange you own 85% of the outstanding stock. No gain is included in income on the exchange of property. However, you recognize ordinary income of $3,000 as payment for services you rendered to the corporation.

Property of relatively small value. The term *property* does not include property of a relatively small value when it is compared to the value of stock and securities already owned or to be received for services by the transferor if the main purpose of the transfer is to qualify for the non-recognition of gain or loss by other transferors.

Property transferred will not be considered to be of relatively small value if its fair market value is at least 10% of the fair market value of the stock and securities already owned or to be received for services by the transferor.

Stock received in disproportion to property transferred. If a group of transferors exchange property for corporate stock, each transferor does not have to receive stock in proportion to his or her interest in the property transferred. If a disproportionate transfer takes place, it will be treated for tax purposes in accordance with its true nature. It may be treated as if the stock were first received in proportion and then some of it used to make gifts, pay compensation for services, or satisfy the transferor's obligations.

Money or other property received. If, in an otherwise nontaxable exchange of property for corporate stock, you also receive money or property other than stock, you may have a taxable gain. You are taxed only up to the amount of money plus the fair market value of the other property you receive. The rules for figuring the taxable gain in this situation generally follow those for a partially nontaxable exchange. If the property you give up includes depreciable property, the taxable gain may have to be reported as ordinary income because of depreciation. No loss is recognized.

Nonqualified preferred stock. Nonqualified preferred stock is treated as property other than stock. Generally, it is preferred stock with any of the following features.

- The holder has the right to require the issuer or a related person to redeem or buy the stock

- The issuer or a related person is required to redeem or buy the stock

- The issuer or a related person has the right to redeem the stock and, on the issue date, it is more likely than not that the right will be exercised

- The dividend rate on the stock varies with reference to interest rates, commodity prices, or similar indices

For a detailed definition of nonqualified preferred stock, see section 351(g)(2) of the Internal Revenue Code.

Liabilities. If the corporation assumes your liabilities the exchange is not generally treated as if you received money or other property. There are two exceptions to this treatment.

- If the liabilities the corporation assumes are more than your adjusted basis in the property you transfer, gain is recognized up to the amount of the difference. However, if the liabilities assumed give rise to a deduction when paid, such as a trade account payable or interest, no gain is recognized.

- If there is no good business reason for the corporation to assume your liabilities, or if your main purpose in the exchange is to avoid federal income tax, the assumption is treated as if you received money in the amount of the liabilities.

For more information on the assumption of liabilities, see section 357(d) of the Internal Revenue Code.

Example. You transfer property to a corporation for stock. Immediately after the transfer you are in control of the corporation. You also receive $10,000 in the exchange. Your adjusted basis in the transferred property is $20,000. The stock you receive has a fair market value of $16,000. The corporation also assumes a $5,000 mortgage on the property for which you are personally liable. Gain is realized as follows.

Fair market value of stock received	$16,000
Cash received	$10,000
Liability assumed by corporation	$ 5,000
Total received	$31,000
Minus: Adjusted basis of property transferred	-$20,000
Realized gain	$11,000

The liability assumed is not treated as money or other property. The recognized gain is limited to $10,000, the amount of cash received.

Loss on exchange. If you have a loss from an exchange and own, directly or indirectly, more than 50% of the corporation's stock, you cannot deduct the loss. This is true even if you do not control the corporation (own less than 80% of its stock).

Basis of stock or other property received. The basis of the stock you receive is generally the adjusted basis of the property you transfer. Increase this amount by any amount that was treated as a dividend, plus any gain recognized on the exchange. Decrease this amount by any cash you received, the fair market value of any other property you received, and any loss recognized on the exchange. Also decrease this amount by the amount of any liability the corporation assumed from you, unless payment of the liability gives rise to a deduction when paid. The basis of any other property you receive is its fair market value on the date of the trade.

Basis of property transferred. A corporation that receives property from you in exchange for its stock generally has the same basis you had in the property increased by any gain you recognized on the exchange. However, the increase for the gain recognized may be limited.

REAL ESTATE IN ANOTHER STATE

Nevada corporations can own real estate in any state in the country without having to register with that particular state. As long as the corporation is not buying and selling properties frequently in a particular state and region, real estate may be bought and sold without many restrictions. Corporations can save lots of money this way considering that some states like California charge out of state registration fees exceeding $1200.

PROTECTING PERSONAL SAVINGS

If you are trying to protect money you have in the bank, here is an important strategy you may want to consider. A bill recently passed by Congress limits FDIC insurance to total deposits of $100,000 for all individual bank accounts, despite the number of accounts held.

Until now, you have been able to spread money out, putting money not just in different branches, but also in different banks altogether. Under this new law the dispersal of funds allowed for FDIC insurance to be applied to each account up to $100,000. One strategy to help protect your money better, includes setting up one new Nevada corporation for each $100,000 that you have. In essence, it is inexpensive insurance.

CORPORATE ESTATE PLANNING

Moving your estate into your corporation is very advantageous with Nevada corporations. We will take a look at how you pass your estate to your families without probate and attorney's costs through corporations. Many approaches to family estate planning are legitimate, and often effective ways of preserving family estates, but consider the rapidly changing tax and legal trends when looking to preserve a lifetime of hard-earned assets. When planning your estate (especially sizable ones), you should assemble competent legal and accounting teams to coordinate proper documentation.

Planning for the next generation is important. Currently the value of your estate that can be transferred to your heirs tax-free is $675,000 and will gradually increase during the next couple of years to $1,000,000. Keep in mind that at any time Congress can change this rule. If a Democratic administration takes place it has been said they would like to change this to $200,000. After this unified credit that we receive, the taxes on the remaining range from 18% to 55%. Some individuals think there is no way their estate would be subject to the estate tax because it's only for the extremely wealthy. Think again; just add up the value of all your assets, real estate, cash, jewelry, bank accounts, brokerage accounts AND the value of your life insurance. The life insurance is tax-free but the value is added into your estate value for determining estate taxes. Start making plans, because there are creative, preventative measures to keep the government out of your pocket.

When working with an estate, you want to start by transferring real property into the corporation to protect those assets from probate. Another way to handle this is to use something as simple as a *living trust*. Your personal assets are always changing. Living trusts should be set up by an attorney and range in price up to $3,000 depending on the complexity of your estate. The living trust will hold your assets such as bank accounts, real estate and other personal items. Keep in mind that living trusts will allow you to *avoid probate, NOT estate taxes*.

GIFTING

Transferring the ownership and control of a corporation to your heirs should be started before you get into an estate tax problem. The simplest way to start doing this is to begin a gifting program to your heirs. You can gift to each heir corporate stock worth $10,000 and if there are two people who own a corporation, they can both give $10,000 each to every heir. This process can be repeated every year.

Long-term corporate planning is not just estate planning. Estate planning alone normally begins when one contemplates death. Such planning has tax implications and interpretations by the IRS that simply don't apply here. If you have done your long-term corporate planning, then you have successfully accomplished a dynamic feat. With your long-term corporate planning, little exists for a lawyer to do. Legal expenses or taxes don't consume your estate. This is why some lawyers are not going to tell you how to take advantage of long-term corporate planning. It is bad for their business. What is the key? Corporations are perpetual unless terminated by statute or by its corporate articles. Corporations do not cease to exist because officers or stockholders die.

Here is an example of long term corporate planning. This type of strategy is referred to as advanced corporate strategy. The sequence in this long-term corporate planning strategy is important, so follow closely:

First you establish a corporation called a shelf corporation. It has no assets and no liabilities. The stock is worthless at this point. Because it has no assets yet, stock from the corporation can be sold to your investors or heirs at one cent per share divided by the prorated amounts you choose, depending on how you want to give to your heirs. Since the stock has been sold to them, it is not a gift. One object of all stock is to increase in value over a period of time. If the stock increases in value, nothing illegal, unethical or strange has occurred. Take a proxy from your stockholders, or your heirs, in this case that allows you to hold the stock even though you don't own it. The proxy may be irrevocable so that your right to vote is guaranteed. In Nevada, a proxy must be renewed every seven years. To ensure its renewal, the shareholders should give you an option to buy the shares back at the initial price of one cent per share. The option can be worded in such a way as to expire upon your death so it wouldn't go through probate. Then put your assets into the corporation.

Some ways of placing assets into a corporation include: Giving assets to the corporation as a capital contribution on behalf of the shareholders. This would be a gift to the shareholders, but if you are within the tax exclusion limits, that is no problem. So again, that has to be broken down to $10,000 per individual. Put your assets into the corporation for a lifetime management contract where you agree to provide certain services for the corporation and the corporation agrees to provide you with a house, all living expenses, plus medical care. This can be an attractive option. You'll want to have a lawyer draw that up properly because the IRS could come in and scrutinize the paperwork.

Another idea is to put assets into the corporation in exchange for a promissory note with interest payments of *interest only* for ten years, and larger installments on principal and *interest after* ten years. The note will expire upon your death. The note could also be a demand note that expires upon your demise. So again, you can put your assets in, get some return on them, and before you die the note expires and it ends up with your heirs. You can control all of your assets but your heirs own them before your demise. No probate, no estate taxes, and no hassles. When you put your assets into the corporation, the value of its stock increases, but there are no taxes until such time as the corporation pays dividends or the stock is sold. In both cases, you have complete control over the matter and can adequately plan in advance to legally avoid taxes.

VOTING VS. NON-VOTING STOCK

Another way of transferring ownership is to move your assets into the corporation. If you place your estate in a corporation you can then give the shares of stock to your heirs, with rights to vote on those shares, by proxy. Another idea is to sell them non-voting common stock of the corporation and you would control all the voting shares. They have their stock in non-voting shares and upon your death, whatever percentage you have left, would then be passed to them and they would have the voting shares broken down between them.

PLAN FOR TOMORROW TODAY!

Most individuals hesitate to transfer assets to their children because they don't want to lose control of those assets or they may be concerned as to how those children are going to manage the assets. By being creative, you can give the assets to the children (for future benefits) without their interference until your percentage of the assets are released at the time of your death. You can secure your assets for the future with proper planning, so start today.

YOUR PAPER TRAIL/YOUR EVIDENCE

When you begin to use some of these corporate strategies, you must be sure that you do not let your record keeping slip. Be sure to plan out your corporate objectives and create the proper documentation. Resolutions, promissory notes, or contracts must be drawn up. There is no reason to risk all that you have developed with your corporation by allowing your corporate veil to be pierced.

CHAPTER 8
THE CORPORATE FORTRESS, HOW TO KEEP IT STRONG

CORPORATE FORMALITIES

What Are They? Maintaining complete and accurate documentation and carrying out the business formalities without fail is imperative to protect the corporate shield from being broken. Formalities are procedures of documentation that track the corporation's thought and activity process. More specifically, the formalities in the form of corporate resolutions, amendments, notes, and meeting minutes of activities conducted. Assembling these forms within the corporate record book legitimizes the business conducted by validating their appropriateness, authenticity, and authorization.

Why Keep Them? Corporate formalities are generally necessitated by a practice called "piercing the corporate veil." Piercing the corporate veil refers to a procedure which occurs during litigation when lawyers attempt to make corporate representatives personally responsible for corporate matters and liabilities. Although it is virtually impossible to pierce the corporate veil in Nevada, in many states, improperly handled corporate formalities are justification enough to hold individuals accountable.

To emphasize just how serious Nevada is about protecting the liability of individuals, let's look at an excerpt from Stephen Presser's 1994 edition of, *Piercing The Corporate Veil*. Presser's book explains the difficulties lawyers often face when attempting to pierce the corporate veil in Nevada. Most difficulties in piercing that veil are attributed to Nevada's three-part test that must be proven in order to assert that the corporation is merely an "alter ego" of its representatives. The three requirements are as follows:

1. The corporation must be influenced and governed by the person asserted to be the alter ego.

2. There must be such unity of interest and ownership that one is inseparable from the other.

3. The facts must be such that adherence to the corporate fiction of a separate entity would, under the circumstances, sanction fraud or promote injustice.

The burden of proof for this test rests with the plaintiff. All three parts to the test must be proven to succeed; failure to prove any one of the three requirements, means failure to pierce the veil. Nevada clearly is dedicated to protecting your security and privacy as individuals. Presser's book covers statutes and case law from every state in the country amounting to almost 900 pages—only seven of which discuss Nevada's alter ego doctrine.

CORPORATE STRUCTURE

Understanding the roles of stockholders, directors, officers, and employees are crucial to the structure of any corporation. Individuals interested in privacy need to pay close attention to their changing roles. Depending on the business at hand or function needed to carry out by a particular office, your role will change often. For example, one week you may be the vice president, and the next week you may be chairman of the board of directors to have the authority to sign an important resolution. Every position in the corporate structure is different and usually corresponds with specific corporate tasks and responsibilities. We will now look at detailed descriptions of each particular office and their duties as well as their places in the overall corporate structure.

The corporate hierarchy basically starts off with a new corporate entity, often referred to as a "shell". Those with the most control and power within the corporate structure reside at the top of the hierarchy—the stockholders or owners of the corporation. The stockholders are responsible for appointing themselves to the board of directors to establish corporate policy and direction.

In Nevada, the board of directors only requires one individual to compose the entire membership of this elite group. More than one may of course serve on the board of directors if they meet the criteria, but this attribute allows one individual total control over a corporation's direction. The majority of corporations have anywhere from 2 to 100 directors serving on the board. The stockholders, based on their abilities to represent the corporation's best interests, appoint directors.

Directors implement the policies of the corporation's yearly and quarterly agendas. They establish financial policies according to the corporation's pre-established goals. Directors elect annual officers who will serve the roles of the president, secretary, and treasurer of the corporation, as well as any other officers or agents deemed necessary. Their decisions are made based on the experience and expertise of the potential officers.

Responsibilities of the officers are to carry out the vision of the board of directors. Officers plan and execute the day-to-day responsibilities of running the corporation. Immediate management issues of the corporation are determined by the officers implementing day-to-day policies. The directors are not generally involved in the day-to-day activities of the corporation, but in Nevada corporations, one person often assumes more than one or all roles in a corporation. Documentation is important to keep in mind when wearing many hats. To learn more about the roles within the corporate structure, look at the "Nevada Revised Statutes" section in the back of the book. These statutes establish the guidelines every corporation must follow according to Nevada law. Reviewing this information will expand your knowledge of how a corporation is regulated and legitimized by the state of Nevada.

Various corporate resolutions and agreements will be featured on the pages that follow, as examples of the documents needed to elect corporate officers and specify their duties.

ANNUAL MEETINGS

Nevada laws require that all corporations have annual stockholders' and director's meetings. Aside from annual fees, this is the only other requirement imposed by the state to keep the corporation in good standing.

You may order a record book from Nevada Corporate Headquarters which will provide you with generic sets of stockholders' and director's meeting minutes that can be easily modified or you can create your own. Regardless, you may want to include inserts of any updates to major meeting decisions (meeting minutes) in your record book for documentation purposes.

Before we get into the minutes, keep in mind that every stockholder and every director must first receive a formal notice or agree to waive their right to formal notice. This is also required every year before the meeting occurs. In the Nevada Revised Statutes section 78.370, it states that a notice must be delivered personally or by postage paid mail. The notice must be given not less than ten days before the meeting and not more than 60 days before the meeting. If one person controls the corporation and fills all the positions of the corporation they can sign a simple waiver to give notice.

The annual stockholder's meeting usually involves a review of the past year's financial situation, a report by the chairman of the board about the plans for the coming year and a vote for the next year's board of directors.

The annual board of directors meeting generally involves a review of the past year, special reports by directors, nominations of next year's officers and a plan for the next year's growth.

Essentially, we have covered all of the territory that is required to be documented annually for the corporation. Again, specifics can be entered into the meeting minutes if someone so chooses, but this essentially is all you need. Your corporate records can be kept simple; they just need to be done.

Our meeting minutes showed that our meeting took place in Las Vegas. As an option to a corporation, the corporation can decide to have its annual meeting absolutely anywhere even though you're in Europe, Hawaii, or elsewhere. Many corporations send their directors all over the country; all over the world. They get paid to attend, they get a vacation, and they get taken care of. It is kind of a fringe benefit for serving the corporation because generally they are not paid a lot of money to serve as directors. This is all a direct expense of the corporation.

Bylaws

Corporate bylaws set out specific structure of a corporation. They are created and adopted by the board of directors of the corporation. They set forth the procedure of operations for the corporate representatives and the roles and responsibilities of each party related to the corporation.

Any specific boundaries that you wish the corporation or its representatives to be bound by can be set forth in the corporate bylaws. The bylaws give the corporation an operating framework to work within. Any matters not specifically adopted in the bylaws of the corporation should then be set forth in corporate resolution and approved meeting minutes. Every child should have guidelines and boundaries, which is essentially what the bylaws represent.

Minutes and Resolutions

You will find that for your own corporate protection and security, you may want to have a lot of paperwork in your corporate record books. It is a good idea to document all that you wish to accomplish and what you have accomplished. Sometimes you may find that it pays to wait until the end of the year, to reconstruct some things and see what it is you want in those records to cover you if anyone comes in to verify your records.

There are two basic ways to manage unordinary functions of a corporation with documentation. One way is through meeting minutes, which are similar in format to the First Meeting Minutes. Directors and stockholders can have minutes of a meeting that took place with someone that took notes as the meeting progressed. This is usually the role of the secretary. The other alternative, which is the more simple way of corporate record management, is to create a document called a corporate resolution. Resolutions are a lot easier.

With a corporate resolution, a physical meeting does not have to actually take place. Each director or stockholder must sign this resolution acknowledging that a certain proposal is approved. By signing the resolution each stockholder or director is putting their approval on it. Corporate resolutions are the easiest way to manage and document a corporation's actions as opposed to someone taking notes and typing out an entire meeting that has taken place. Just state the specifics of what you are trying to accomplish. Both directors and stockholders can handle corporate affairs through resolutions, but generally it is the directors that hold the meetings that decide changes or significant business of a corporation.

The following pages have various resolutions for you to review and gain a better idea of their format and their use. This first resolution is the general format that all resolutions can be formatted from. You will see this format in every resolution. There are three or more parts to every resolution. The format begins with the directors announcing the resolution. In the middle of every resolution is the meat that tells what actually is being proposed and what the decision is. The last part is the date of the resolution and the signatures of the directors or the stockholders. Corporate resolutions are usually typed but they can also be handwritten or kept in a computer.

One thing to keep in mind with your corporate resolutions or meeting minutes is that they can be created after the fact. It is a simple practice of creating corporate resolutions once something has occurred. This way you know why it was created, exactly who did it, when it happened, and what actually occurred. Then you can go back and create the necessary paperwork that describes you approving the activity taking place. Postdate these resolutions as long as something did take place. In a legal situation, corporations that did not properly keep good records all of the time suddenly find that their corporations are full of records just in the nick of time.

Resolutions don't have to be as formally written as we have put them together, but you want to be sure that your focus is clear and concise so as not to confuse anyone who may read it. The attorneys have put their language, often referred to as "legalese", into far too many things today. This language, which is taught in the law schools around the country, only seems to confuse most people - which is obviously its intent.

YOUR ROLE AS "CONTROLLER"

Now we will discuss your relationship and responsibilities to the corporation. The best way to think about your affiliation with the corporation is that it is an entity separate and distinct from yourself. In other words, you really don't have a corporation at all. Refer to the corporation as "the entity I work for", "the entity I am contracted with" or "the entity I do business with." On the other hand, DO NOT refer to the entity as "MY corporation"; keep this in mind at all times. Do not disclose any information about your control or ownership of the corporation to individuals to whom you are affiliated. Separate yourself from the corporate identity. Be sure to be conscious of the language you use around colleagues and business acquaintances to reflect the relationship to the corporation that you prefer. Too often, too many people, because of ignorance or ego, share their personal affairs with others. But exposing information may hurt you in the future, so keep your affiliation with the corporation private.

PLAYING THE GAME

Your relationship to the corporation is, in essence, a role-playing game. Your role can and more than likely will change often depending on the business at hand. Think of your role similar to the one James Garner played in that old television show, *Rockford Files*. In the show, the main character would have to assume professional titles in order to solve the case. One day he would be the president of a major company then the next day he would present himself as a humble phone repairman. Essentially, you must wear many different hats. One day you will need to be the corporation's business manager to carry out certain duties, while another day, you might need to present yourself as the president of the corporation to close a big sale. Many different situations will arise requiring you to play different roles within the corporate structure.

Flexibility is key when taking on these different roles and tasks. Occasionally, in order to sign a certain document, you will need to be an elected officer. It is important that you maintain accurate and sufficient documentation to support the changes in your role when required. Making contracts and getting into business dealings should be simple procedures if carried out correctly. Simply choose a title that will best facilitate a task and document the change within your corporate records.

The more you practice this game in your day to day corporate routine, the easier it will be to verify your relationship to the corporation, should you become involved in litigation. Preserving your distance from the corporation will help prevent anyone from piercing the corporate veil. Remember, YOU are not the corporation. If you are ever called onto a witness stand you need to have your relationship to the corporation very clear in your mind so that you do not hesitate to answer the questions accurately.

If you set up your corporation correctly, you can feel confident that you are literally telling the absolute truth. If privacy is a concern of yours, make sure to issue bearer shares so that you will never have to disclose ownership because by law you will not own the corporation. With bearer shares, the only way to honestly say you are the owner of the corporation is if you have all the shares issued in your name or if you hold the bearer shares in your hand. Although this information may seem redundant, the importance of your relationship to the corporation is pertinent. Always remember that your corporation is a separate and distinct entity from yourself. You are not it. It is not you.

KEEPING AT ARM'S LENGTH

Part of keeping at arm's length from the corporation means that you must take precautions to preserve a legitimate distance from the corporation. In order to validate separating yourself from the corporation, you need to make sure that you carry business out legitimately. Hint: do not commingle funds. Many people think it is okay to pay for small personal items or an outing here or there with corporate funds—after all the corporation's money is really your money, right? Wrong. Again, bad habits could have serious consequences in the future. Just as you are separate from the corporation, your money is separate from corporation money as well. Merging your money will supply strong evidence to anyone interested in piercing the corporate veil by simply proving that the corporation is simply an alter ego of yourself.

Although it is necessary to separate yourself from the corporation, the fact is that any endeavor requires money. Unless you have a slew of investors anxious to hand over their money, chances are that the start-up capital will have to come from your pocket. But remember that your generosity alone is not enough to justify giving the corporation a large sum of money to get started. In this day and age, compensation is the keyword—what's in it for me? This should be the question on your mind because it will be the question on others' minds should your motivation for giving the money ever be questioned.

One way to give the corporation money is through a capital contribution in exchange for stock. Although this would not be ideal for those wanting anonymity, this is a simple and effective way to fund the corporation. The value of the stock increases with the additional capital formation. Start-up capital is non-taxable income, so invest your money wisely.

Another way to move money around is to give a loan to the corporation. In exchange for the funding you give to the corporation, the corporation provides you with a promissory note with specific pay back terms including interest acquired over time. The pay back period may not be immediate; it could be given years from the time of the loan, but again, being sure that the compensation is reasonable.

Regardless of how the transaction takes place, documentation and compensation of that exchange is key. There must always be a legitimate business reason to support transactions between the corporation and you. But strategies can be very creative as well. For example, if you are interested in purchasing a piece of property, buying a new car, or taking a vacation, you still can—but you must act according to legitimate business reasons. Actually, keep in mind that the items purchased will not be "yours" per se, but rather you are able to access these items as an employee, agent or affiliate of the corporation. So, let's say that the corporation purchases a corporate car and you, as the vice president, carry out important duties on behalf of the business, and consequently, need a car to drive. Although the corporation is formally registered under the corporate name and owned by that entity, you are allowed to drive the vehicle as a condition of your position with the business. You have just established a legitimate business reason to drive the corporate car. The same basic concept can be applied to taking a vacation (by having a meeting during your trip) or buying a piece of property (for the corporation's future investment). The more creative you are the better—but you need accurate and complete documentation to support these decisions.

Part of providing complete documentation is to make sure those resolutions, checks and other important forms are accurately filled out. It is absolutely necessary to sign the documents with the proper title when you authorize corporate decisions. Let's say you want to buy a piece of property on the corporation's behalf. You authorize the purchase of property, make a resolution, write a check for the given amount and sign it with your name. Transaction complete, right? Wrong. By forgetting to sign with BOTH your name and your TITLE, you have just made a serious mistake. By forgetting to identify your authority to sign such a form, you have subjected the corporation to severe scrutiny. In fact, for such a simple and seemingly insignificant mistake, the corporation may very well be pierced by validating the speculation of its alter-ego status in relation to you.

Procedures are very important. But just because you cannot buy your groceries with the corporate debit card does not mean that the corporation will not end up paying for your food—all for a legitimate business reason. Perhaps at the end of the month, the corporation will write the vice president an allowance check. This check can then be cashed and then food may be purchased at the market. In this way the corporation may compensate contractors, employees, and officers for all their service and hard work. Individuals that happen to work with or for Nevada corporations, but live outside the state, may redeem even more compensation because of the distance, additional time given, or general hassles of working for a company out of state.

SPECIAL ROLE OF THE VICE PRESIDENT

Considering that most people incorporate in Nevada to preserve their privacy, its no surprise that the special role of the vice president is used so frequently in incorporations today. Vice presidents have the unique advantage of being able to maintain complete control over corporate affairs while keeping their anonymity as well. As discussed earlier, state provisions make this special role possible. The Annual List of Officers does not require the vice president to disclose his/her name for the public record. Instead, only the offices of the president, secretary, treasurer and director are required. In Nevada, all of the remaining positions may be filed with the name of just one individual. Those who want to lower their public profile can take advantage of this fact by electing a nominee officer to represent the corporation on the Secretary of State of Nevada's public records. Nevada Corporate Headquarters (NCH) provides such a service to its customers, for a reasonable amount, providing clients with assurance that they can maintain complete control over corporate affairs and have privacy too.

Vice presidents can remain silent in the background while watching their ideas materialize. Two documents make this possible. One is the nominee officer contract agreement between NCH and yourself withdrawing any and all involvement or obligation to the day-to-day decisions of the corporation. This contract protects NCH from any liability the corporation may incur and the clients from the involvement of the nominee officer. It's just a straightforward business transaction—services in exchange for payment. The second item is included in the corporate bylaws. The bylaws stipulate that the vice president is responsible for representing and carrying out the duties of the president in his/her absence. Hiring an nominee office in this case would leave the presidency absent, requiring the vice president to step in and take charge of all corporate matters. To further protect the owners of the corporation, amendments to the original articles of incorporation could be filed as well—stripping the officers on the state list of any power.

Remember that there is no risk for you as an officer when you fill in for the president (with the exception of fraudulent activities) according to the state and reflected more specifically in the articles of incorporation, Article VIII and IX.

Business License

It is a requirement that all Nevada corporations acquire a state business license from the Department of Taxation. This license is used to collect a tax on each employee in the state. All corporations that have employees in the State of Nevada must pay a $25 tax per employee every three months (fees are subject to change; please check with your resident agent). If your corporation will not have any employees working in the state of Nevada, this form will be filed with a one-time fee of $25 (again, subject to change). There is no annual fee thereafter, unless new employees are hired in the future.

Nevada Seller's Permit (Resale Number)

If your corporation is selling a product or any tangible items within the state of Nevada, it is a state requirement that your corporation obtain a state Seller's Permit. A state Seller's Permit number will allow your corporation to purchase supplies to be sold by your corporation without having to pay tax on those items, as long as they are for resale. With a Resale Number, you are required to charge the appropriate sales tax on items that you sell. These taxes are collected by your corporation and paid to the state of Nevada. The state will provide the appropriate form for your corporation. Simply call the State of Nevada Department of Taxation at (702) 687-4820.

CHAPTER 9
BUILDING A
POWERFUL CORPORATION

FIRST STEP

The first step to setting up and using your corporation is putting the documentation and corporate record book together. A software program has been recently developed that makes this task painless. The software CorporateManagerCD is available by going to **www.corporatemanagercd.com.** The software is set up as a corporate record book and has hundreds of agreements, resolutions and paperwork that every corporation needs to track. The advantage of this software is that you can track multiple corporations, there is a common activities section for documentation and you will never have to deal with paper again. It is a great tool and highly recommend.

CORPORATE RESPONSIBILITIES

The following descriptions of corporate officer and director responsibilities comes from the Revised Statutes of Nevada.

DIRECTORS

Let's look at section 78120: *The Board of Director's General Powers:* The board of directors is only subject to limitations as may be provided by this chapter or the articles of incorporation. The board of directors fully controls the affairs of the corporation. The bylaws included in the corporate record book further discuss the responsibilities and limited liability of the directors and officers of a corporation.

Getting back to the Nevada statutes, section 78125: *Committees of the Board of Directors, Designations, Powers, Names and Memberships* indicates the following: The board of directors is an entity that represents a corporation, but has the authority to delegate the responsibilities to committees that carry out the duties. In Nevada, they have the right to designate any responsibility to non-board members to assist the board of directors.

OFFICERS

Now let's jump over to section 78130 of NRS: *Officers of Corporation, Selections, Terms, and Duties*. Now we are going to get into some of the responsibilities of the president, secretary, treasurer and any vice presidents of the corporation. It says here that every corporation in Nevada must have a president, secretary, and treasurer. These officers are chosen by the board of directors and hold their offices until qualified successors are chosen. Number two says every corporation may have one or more vice presidents, assistant secretaries, assistant directors and any such other officers and agents as may be deemed necessary. You may choose to fill any office at any time. Make sure that the proper paperwork is drawn up for the new officers or directors the corporation hires.

Number three says that all officers and agents must be chosen according to specific guidelines, hold offices for specified terms, and fulfill powers as described by the bylaws or determined by the board of directors. In other words, all decisions and actions made on behalf of the corporation must be documented. Burying corporate proceedings in paperwork is a good idea in case the IRS or other probing groups want to pry into your business.

Authority of the Directors. Any contract conveyance otherwise lawful, made in the name of the corporation, which is authorized to ratify by the directors or is done within the scope of the authority, actual or apparent, given by the directors, binds the corporation and the corporation acquires the rights there under. So, remember that anything you sign is binding. You are locked in to the agreement.

The next section we will look at is 78138: *Directors and Officers* referring to the exercise of powers and performance of duties.

1. Directors and officers shall exercise their powers in alignment with the interests of the corporation. In performing their responsive duties, directors and officers are entitled to rely on information, opinions, reports, books of accounts or statements including financial statements and other financial data that are prepared or presented by one or more of the directors, counsels, public accountants, and committees appointed by the directors to represent them.

2. Directors and officers, when exercising their powers in alignment with the interests of the corporation may also consider the interests of the employees, suppliers, creditors, customers, the economy of the state and nation, the community and society, and the long and short-term interests of the corporation.

Remember, your responsibility is to preserve the life and longevity of the corporation.

Directors may resist change or potential change in the control of the corporation if the directors are a quorum and agree by majority vote that the change is not in alignment with the interests of the corporation. Refer to section "B" in section 78138 stating, " . . . because of the amount or nature of the indebtedness or other obligations to which the corporation are in successor to the party of either may become subject to in connection with the change or the potential change in control, provides reasonable grounds to believe that within a reasonable time, the assets of the corporation or any successor would be or become less than the liabilities." This section describes the responsibilities of the officers and directors with respect to a corporation that is failing. The directors and officers must act in accordance with what is best for the corporation.

Please take the time to familiarize yourself with the Nevada Revised Statutes presented at the end of this book. Note that what is not stated in the statutes may be clarified in Nevada Case Law. Consult a Nevada attorney for more specifics.

CORPORATE FORMALITIES CHECKLIST

When an individual gets ready to incorporate there are many business related matters on their mind. After incorporating, the individuals move full speed ahead into marketing and creating revenue for the new entity. Often months roll by before they take an opportunity to make sure all the proper steps have been taken in keeping the corporation updated and bulletproof. Below is a list of questions to ask of the corporation upon incorporating to increase the awareness of the necessary tasks that are required now and in the future. I strongly recommend referring to this list every three months.

1. Have you chosen a resident agent for the corporation?   Yes___ No___

2. Do you fully understand the articles of the corporation?   Yes___ No___

3. Do you fully understand the bylaws of the corporation?   Yes___ No___

4. Do you know how many sharers of stock were authorized?   Yes___ No___

5. Do you know what the par value of the shares were?   Yes___ No___

6. Have you signed an acceptance of the appropriate officer positions in the corporate record book? (Including positions of director, president, vice president, secretary and treasurer).   Yes___ No___

7. Have you had your first board of directors meeting?   Yes___ No___

8. Has the secretary signed the acceptance of the bylaws?   Yes___ No___

9. Have the appropriate officers signed the resolution to the board of directors? Yes___ No___

10. Has the contract with an independent contractor been signed?   Yes___ No___

11. Has the corporation decided on the fiscal year?   Yes___ No___

12. Has the corporation decided to elect "S" status   Yes___ No___
    (A corporation has 75 days from the date of incorporation to select "S" status)
    or remain a "C" corporation?

13. Has the corporation issued stock?   Yes___ No___

14. Has the corporation recorded this in the stock register?   Yes___ No___

15. Has the corporation obtained a Tax I.D. Number?   Yes___ No___

16. Has the stock ledger statement been filled out by the secretary of the   Yes___ No___
    corporation and sent to the corporation's resident agent?

17. Have the bylaws of the corporation been adopted?   Yes___ No___

18. Has a copy of the bylaws and articles been sent to the resident agent?   Yes___ No___

19. Was the corporate resolution filed to issue the corporate stock?   Yes___ No___

20. Does the corporation have to qualify in another state?   Yes___ No___

21. Has the corporation obtained a state business license?   Yes___ No___

22. Has the corporation filed the initial list of officers?   Yes___ No___

23. If your corporation is over a year old, have you had an annual meeting of   Yes___ No___
    the board of directors?

24. If the corporation is over a year old, have you paid your yearly resident   Yes___ No___
    agent fees?

25. If your corporation is over a year old, have you filed the annual   Yes___ No___
    list of officers?

26. Have you given proper notice or used the appropriatenotice for all   Yes___ No___
    meetings of stockholders and directors?

27. Have corporate resolutions been utilized by the board of directors to   Yes___ No___
    authorize and document all major corporate acts?

28. Has the corporate bank account been properly established?   Yes___ No___

29. Have the corporate books been kept separate from personal transactions   Yes___ No___
    to avoid commingling of funds?

30. Has a CPA professional been chosen to help guide the corporation process?   Yes___ No___

31. Has the corporation kept receipts for all businessexpenses?   Yes___ No___

32. Are the appropriate independent contractors agreements drawn up?   Yes___ No___

33. Have the proper promissory notes been drawn up?   Yes___ No___

34. Have DBAs been filed?   Yes___ No___

35. Have you attended any informational workshops to increase your corporate knowledge?   Yes___ No___

Ideally, the corporation should answer yes to all of these questions if they are applicable. If this is not the case, I recommend setting some time aside to accomplish these points. Hopefully, the corporation will never have to face a million-dollar lawsuit, if it does; these are the basic steps that need to be taken immediately to keep the corporations veil from being pierced.

ISSUING STOCK

A corporation is owned by its shareholders. Shareholders make a contribution to the corporation in the form of cash, notes, tangible or intangible property, stock and anything else of value, in a free exchange for shares of ownership (also called "stock shares"), in proportion to the accepted value of the property they contributed. Multiple owners usually agree on the value of any non-cash contributions, but single owners merely put in what they need to operate and are issued 100 percent of the issued shares in return.

As the value of a corporation increases, so too does the value of each share of the corporation's stock. Any additional assets placed into a corporation by its owners will increase the value of the shares in the corporation. The value of a corporation's shares is calculated by determining the difference between a corporation's assets and it liabilities, plus the value of the "good will" of the corporation, divided by the number of issued shares of the corporation.

Every corporation is authorized to issue a certain number of shares of stock. This authorization number of shares is set in the Articles of Incorporation. Of those authorized shares, the corporation's directors decide how many shares they will issue. A corporation could have 2,500 shares authorized and only have issued one share of stock. That one share of stock would then make up the entire ownership of the corporation. A corporation's ownership is only based on those shares of the corporation's stock that have been issued.

Because Nevada keeps the ownership of a corporation a private matter by not asking for any information regarding the corporation's ownership, finding out just who the owner is can become quite difficult. If the IRS or an individual who is filing suit against a corporation is trying to track down a corporation's owner, they will start with the resident agent's office. The resident agent will acknowledge that they represent that corporation. In order to get the documentation that the resident agent has on file (the articles, bylaws and stock ledger statement), there must be a court order to retrieve those documents from the resident agent. This starts them on the trail to the corporation record book, because the document called the "stock ledger statement" tells where the stock ledger, (located in the record book) is kept. The stock ledger should reflect whom the shares of the corporation have been issued to. If your shares have never been issued, it doesn't say anything; but if they catch up with the corporate record book, they have basically caught up with the owner of the corporation, especially if the shares have never been filled out. Even if they weren't filled out but are in your possession, a judge, because of bearer shares in Nevada, will say that you are the owner of the corporation. If somebody got on the trail of the corporation and went to the resident agent, the resident agent would notify you that somebody was on the trail of the corporation. The corporate record book (which has the stock ledger in it), could then be moved, transferred or sent somewhere else. It is then the responsibility of the owner of that corporation to provide the resident agent with the new address of where the stock ledger is kept, in the form of a new stock ledger statement.

TYPES OF STOCK

Common Stock. Common stocks are stock shares that usually possess voting rights and are entitled to dividends as declared by the board of directors and to a proportionate share in the distribution of assets at the time of the corporation's liquidation. Because of these ownership characteristics, common stock generally appreciates or depreciates in price according to a corporation's profitability.

Voting Stock. This class of stock allows the holder of the shares a voting right for each share. Control of the corporation resides in these shares.

Non-Voting Stock. These shares are entitled to a portion of the profits, but they represent no control over operations.

Preferred Stock. Preferred stock is a class of stock with a preference over other forms of stock, normally as to dividend, but sometimes as to voting or liquidation rights.

Cumulative Preferred Stock. This is a class of preferred stock that carries with it a guaranteed return. For instance, the stock may pay out a 10 percent annual dividend, but if the company does not have a good year and there are no profits with which to pay this dividend, the 10 percent accumulates into the next year when, hopefully, there will again be profits.

Convertible Preferred Stock. These are preferred shares that allow the owners to still receive a dividend and allow the owner to convert those shares into common shares and participate in the profits of the company.

Bearer Stock. Nevada is the only state left that allows for bearer stock to be used by a corporation. Bearer stock is simply stock that is the general person; i.e., the certificate is made out to Bearer, which means that whoever bears or has possession of the stock certificate is the owner. The fun thing about this type of stock is that it becomes impossible for anyone to track ownership or the transfer of ownership. This is true privacy!

Today's world offers asset protection and privacy challenging each of us to remain sharp and creative. Do not take advice from others blindly. Be skeptical of what others tell you with respect to managing the affairs of the corporation you control. Even your accountants or lawyers may give you incorrect information regarding corporations out of ignorance. Nevada corporate statutes differ from most states in the country and they may just be unaware of the unique advantages Nevada offers. Again, your council may have the best of intentions, but ignorance can be dangerous. The consultants and experts at Nevada Corporate Headquarters, Inc. will be glad to discuss any questions you or your council may have.

BANK ACCOUNTS

Once you are ready to start using your corporation, you will want to set up a bank account. Even if you are not yet in a place to start using your corporation, it is a good idea to have a bank account set up so that when you are ready to begin using your corporation, everything is ready to go. When a corporate strategy involves using a Nevada corporation, even though the owner or representatives of the corporation do not live in Nevada, it is best to establish a Nevada bank account to further legitimize the presence of the corporation in the preferred state. If for convenience, you want a bank account in your home state, there is no problem with that, but make sure that it is IN ADDITION to a Nevada bank account. Remember, that you don't want to defeat the purpose of having a Nevada corporation by cheating yourself out of tax advantages by running transactions through your home state corporation.

When using a home state bank account for your Nevada corporation, it is best to make a deposit in Nevada first and then transfer money, via check, to your home state bank account. This is the cleanest way to end up with corporate funds in your home state to give you access to corporate cash. This process helps solidify your Nevada corporation by primarily operating in Nevada.

A Nevada corporation can open a corporate bank account in every state in this country without having to register for doing business in that particular state. You may run into a few banks that will tell you that you need to be registered in their state, but we have found that most banks are uninformed. If you run into resistance or unnecessary questioning regarding your corporate matters, choose a more cooperative bank.

Establishing a Nevada bank account can, in many respects, be easier than setting one up in your home state. In fact, the corporate account can be set up without ever having to come to Nevada. Nevada Corporate Headquarters, Inc., has established a very friendly relationship with three major Nevada banks for processing corporate bank accounts. Once your Nevada bank account is set up and you have received your bank deposit slips and checks, it is very simple to mail the bank your deposits. The bank will send you a receipt of your deposit or you can call the bank to see deposits posted to the account. Optional services such as on-line banking or NCH's depositing service are other choices you may want to consider as well.

*Note that all interest earned by a corporation is reported annually to the IRS. Therefore, if you desire to keep the IRS as far away as possible, just set up a non-interest bearing checking account for the corporation.

For those of you who are looking to set up a corporate checking account without having to give out your social security number, you may want to consider a mutual fund checking account. There are many mutual funds around the country that offer corporate accounts to hold cash in money market funds allowing the corporation access to those funds via checks. These accounts are simple to set up and they don't want to know very much information. Best of all, they are outside the Federal Reserve System!

FEDERAL EMPLOYER IDENTIFICATION NUMBER (EIN)

Before you walk into a bank to set up your corporate account, you need to apply with the IRS for an Employer Identification Number (EIN—also called a Tax Identification Number). This is essentially your corporate Social Security number. This is the number that the IRS uses to track each and every corporation. The IRS wants to know as much as they can about the corporation and everyone involved in it, so they ask for an individual's social security number in order to obtain the EIN.

For those concerned with privacy, you may want to consider having your resident agent apply for your EIN number on the corporation's behalf. The number would be sent to the resident agent address instead of your own providing a layer of privacy and if you use the nominee officer service, your social security number will not be required.

The form used to apply for the EIN is called the SS-4 form. The quickest way to receive your corporate number is to fax your completed SS-4 form to the IRS. Either fax the IRS in Ogden, Utah at 1-801-620-7115 with a cover page requesting that they fax their reply back to you (your EIN, or Employer Identification Number will be faxed back within five working days) or mail your form to the IRS:

MS 6271-T

P.O. BOX 9950

OGDEN, UT 84409

MONEY

Money is put into a corporation to either fund future activities or, in the case of a small asset protection corporation, money is given to a corporation as a loan. Loans are popular vehicles to move money because they save individuals money by lowering personal tax.

There are primarily two classifications for funds as you place them into your corporation's bank account: capital contributions or loans. Larger corporations will have a third class similar to a loan called *corporate bonds* as well.

A capital contribution means that you are placing money into a corporation as an investor of that corporation. When you place your money into the corporation as an investment, the corporation would then give you shares of stock in the corporation. The number of shares of stock that you receive is based on the value of each share. A share of stock could be valued at any price; it could be worth one dollar or one million dollars.

By loaning money to a corporation you are essentially giving the corporation funds. In exchange, the corporation is going to give you a promissory note. This promissory note would tell you the length of the note and the rate of return (interest) on the note. If the corporation does issue a promissory note for a loan, be sure to create a corporate resolution authorizing the loan.

BROKERAGE ACCOUNTS

A Nevada corporation can open a brokerage account to be utilized for the investment of extra money that the company may be holding. A corporation, like an individual, can invest in anything from U.S. treasury bonds to stock option contracts (a highly speculative investment).

The account opening forms for corporations are a bit more tiresome than the forms for individuals but the end result is the same. Many brokerage firms offer special accounts to businesses to maximize the returns on cash. These accounts offer checking access to funds that are earning very competitive returns in national and international money fund pools. Additionally, many of these accounts come with a credit or debit card when you set up a new account.

CREDIT CARDS

Credit cards for new corporations can be difficult to get. Corporations that don't have any credit history established are very unlikely candidates for corporate credit cards. Some banks will take a look at the credit history of the officers of the corporation and use that as a basis for their decision. If you are considering applying for a card, try American Express; they seem to be on a national campaign to attract new corporate accounts (call 1-800-SUCCESS).

Your corporate profile increases with a credit card but this may be just what you want because it may also greatly reduce your personal profile. If you are dealing with more than one corporation, then the suggestion is to keep one in sound financial shape and one that takes up quite a few corporate losses. Credit cards today are all tied into the international tracking system that is out there. You should only be using your credit cards on things that you absolutely have to, for instance, making reservations in hotels and getting vehicles to rent.

BANK LOANS

Loans for corporations can often be quite difficult to get unless a corporation can consistently show income sufficient to pay the loan back. New corporations are less likely to get bank loans because like a college student just starting off, they will not have much or any kind of credit history.

If you try to get a bank loan with a new corporation, chances are that you as an individual will have to co-sign for the corporation. This is the way many new corporations begin to build depth to their credit history.

CORPORATE RECORD BOOK

This section covers all of the initial documentation in a typical Nevada corporation record book. These are the documents required by Nevada statues to get the corporation moving. These documents place the corporations elected officials in their respective offices. Read through the flow of these documents and you will have a better understanding of what they represent. Remember, you are not the corporation. When the corporation's elected representative makes a significant corporate decision, it should be briefly documented as a corporate resolution. All corporate documentation should be kept together. A three-ring binder works perfectly to keep all of your records protected and in their proper order. Corporate record books with corporate seals can be ordered through your resident agent.

Note regarding banks: Nevada does not require that a corporation have a corporate seal. However, many out-of-state banks and title companies want to see a corporate seal; therefore, we strongly recommend that every corporation have one. Once again, corporate seals can be ordered through your resident agent.

Your corporation's resident agent is required to have three forms on file for your corporation. The first is a copy of the corporation's Articles of Incorporation. The second is the bylaws of the corporation. The third required form is the stock ledger statement, which is the link to your corporation's stockholders. The stock ledger statement tells anyone who presents a court order to your resident agent to view your corporate records exactly where your corporation's list of stockholders is located. A copy of these three sets of documents must be kept on file with your Nevada resident agent.

LIST OF OFFICERS, DIRECTORS, AND AGENT OF FORM

Once the Articles of Incorporation have been filed with the Secretary of State, Nevada will send you a form called a "List of Officers, Directors and Agent Of ..." that you fill out and mail back to them. You must file the list the first day of the second month of incorporation. An $85 check (subject to change; call your resident agent if you are uncertain) is to be included annually with the List of Officers of your corporation, to pay the state's annual filing fee.

The list asks for the name of the president, secretary, treasurer, and directors of the corporation. Included with their names, you must provide an accurate address of the current officers and directors. This List of Officers is a matter of public record. Therefore, anyone wishing to check this information with the Secretary of State's office can do so with one simple phone call.

Please note that the "List of Officers, Directors and Agent Of" form does not ask for the vice president's name(s). This is the time to utilize privacy strategies with your Nevada corporation. We highly recommend the services of Nevada Corporate Headquarters, Inc., a resident agent that is willing to work with you to develop privacy strategies.

Next we have enclosed a copy of the current "List of Officers, Directors and Agent Of" so that you recognize this form when the State of Nevada sends it to you.

FUNDING YOUR CORPORATION

Corporations are usually funded for some future activity or investment. In the case of a small asset-protection corporation, money is placed into a corporation specifically to get the money out of an individual's name.

There are primarily two classifications for funds as you place them into your corporation's bank account. Those funds can be classified as either a capital contribution, or as a loan to the corporation. Larger corporations will have a third class similar to a loan called corporate bonds.

CAPITAL CONTRIBUTIONS

This section explains the tax treatment of contributions from shareholders and non-shareholders.

Paid-in capital. Contributions to the capital of a corporation, whether or not by shareholders, are paid-in capital. These contributions are not taxable to the corporation.

However, contributions to a corporation in aid of construction or any other contribution as a customer or potential customer is taxable to the corporation.

Basis. The basis of property contributed to capital by a shareholder is the same as the basis the shareholder had in the property increased by any gain recognized on the exchange.

The basis of property contributed to capital by a person other than a shareholder is zero.

If a corporation receives a cash contribution from a person other than a shareholder, reduce the basis of property acquired with the money during the 12-month period beginning on the day it received the contribution by the amount of the contribution. If the amount contributed is more than the cost of the property acquired, then reduce, but not below zero, the basis of the other properties held by the corporation on the last day of the 12-month period in the following order.

1. Depreciable property.

2. Amortizable property.

3. Property subject to cost depletion but not to percentage depletion.

4. All other remaining properties.

Reduce the basis of property in each category to zero before going to the next category.

There may be more than one piece of property in each category. Base the reduction of the basis of each property on the ratio of the basis of each piece of property to the total bases of all property in that category. If the corporation wishes to make this adjustment in some other way, it must get IRS consent. The corporation files a request for consent with its income tax return for the tax year in which it receives the contribution.

CHAPTER 10
FINDING A NEVADA HOME

RESIDENT AGENT

According to Nevada Revised Statute - **NRS 78.030** corporations are required to have a resident agent at the time of formation and throughout the duration of the corporation's existence.

> NRS 78.030 **Filing of articles of incorporation and certificate of acceptance of appointment of resident agent.**
>
> 1. One or more persons may establish a corporation for the transaction of any lawful business, or to promote or conduct any legitimate object or purpose, pursuant and subject to the requirements of this chapter, by:
>
> (a) Executing and filing in the office of the secretary of state articles of incorporation; and
>
> (b) Filing a certificate of acceptance of appointment, <u>executed by the resident agent of the corporation</u>, in the office of the secretary of state.

The resident agent location is where any government correspondence or legal documentation is sent. The resident agent is required to hold a copy of the corporation's charter, articles, bylaws and a stock ledger statement. The stock ledger statement indicates where the stock ledger is located. The stock ledger indicates the owners of the corporation.

NEVADA CORPORATE HEADQUARTERS, INC. (NCH)

The author of this book recommends using the services of Nevada Corporate Headquarters, Inc. (NCH). They have formed over 10,000 corporations since 1992 and their primary commitment is to preserve the privacy of their clients.

Use NCH as a diversion for the corporation by solidifying a presence at their location. As your resident agent, NCH will draw attention to the corporation's "headquarters" as much as possible. To firmly establish a legitimate headquarters, the corporation needs to use the physical address of its resident agent.

As part of their responsibilities to the state, resident agents are required to have regular business hours five days a week and to have a location accessible to the general public. Just as resident agents have responsibilities to the state, corporations are required to supply certain information to their resident agent. The specific documentation that must remain in the corporation's file with the resident agent includes: a copy of the articles of incorporation, the bylaws signed by an officer, and stock ledger statement.

Remember, your resident agent is a buffer between the corporation and yourself. Anyone trying to locate you or the corporation must first start with your resident agent. Documents held with your resident agent can be inspected by a shareholder of the corporation with valid identification or by anyone with a court order. If a corporation neglects to use a resident agent, the state of Nevada imposes a fine of $100 to $500 according to state code NRS 78.090. Nevada Revised Statues Section 78.090 through 78.110 spell out the requirements and the functions of your Resident Agent. Some interesting thoughts come up in those sections of the statutes that may be important to those of you who like to test the system.

Section 78.105 goes into the maintenance of records held at the resident agent's office. Section 78.105 (2) states that a corporation must maintain the records required in sub-section one in written form or in another form capable of conversion into written form within a "reasonable" time. This obviously leaves some room for the corporation that does not have the required documentation on hand at the resident agent's office. Now for those of you that are always looking for new ways to test the law, it is possible for a corporation that did not have the required documentation on hand to fax a copy of these documents to the resident agent's office in case of an emergency. This would allow the extreme privacy, but that decision is up to each individual corporation.

Although there are no penalties placed on the resident agent, corporations are subject to fines and penalties by the state if they choose to be negligent. Subsection "S" of Section 78.105 states that:

Every corporation that refuses or neglects to keep the stock ledger or duplicate copy thereof open for inspection, as required in this subsection, shall forfeit to the state the sum of $25 for every day of such neglect or refusal.

This may in some cases be a reasonable fine for corporation's primarily concerned with privacy.

History of NCH

In 1992, I, Cort W. Christie formed Nevada Corporate Headquarters, Inc. as a resident agent in the state of Nevada. Since its inception, NCH, Inc. has grown from a small Resident Agent Service to a nationally recognized corporation. In addition to representing corporations from its offices in Las Vegas, the company also sets up corporations for individuals and provides various services from mail forwarding to complete office packages.

In the past seven years, Nevada Corporate Headquarters, Inc. has come from obscurity to a thriving organization, built on solid principles. There have been many changes to accommodate the vast amount of growth the company has experienced in such a short amount of time. NCH's foundation was established with both the company's prosperity and the best intentions for its clients, personnel and associated businesses in mind. Normally, this growth would depend on loans or overhanging debt. However, NCH, Inc. has reached its status with no debt liability whatsoever. These guidelines have held, and will continue to hold, this resident agent together indefinitely.

Over the years, NCH, Inc. has established itself in the industry as one of the top resident agents in the state of Nevada. Its employees are the reason why. A fully staffed consulting and customer service department is set up to meet your every need. Employees are selected through an intensive screening process that emphasizes their willingness to be of service. Most successful companies have an excellent support staff to which they attribute much of their prosperity— NCH, Inc. is one of them. In order to gain market share and continued growth, an advanced management information system must be present to assist resident agents participating in this industry. From its interactive website and on-line access to the Secretary of the State's database, to its employee usage of an Intranet, the company has achieved a stable, organized environment to handle the ensuing growth. Not only does this environment serve as a quick service provider, but it also gives Nevada Corporate Headquarters, Inc. the edge over the competition when it comes to providing complete client satisfaction.

Reputation

NCH, Inc. has been the corporate structuring specialist for nearly eight years and represents over 10,000 clients worldwide. NCH, Inc. is dedicated to providing the highest standard of customer service to obtain 100% satisfaction for its clients. With over half of all business derived from referrals and its own client base you can see they succeed in doing so.

NCH, Inc. has several highly recognized lawyers, CPAs and financial planners from around the country, who put their trust in NCH to structure corporate strategies for their clients. NCH, Inc. has built a reputation around the country as the specialist in entity structuring to assist the entrepreneur, the large corporations, and the licensed professionals.

NCH is committed to maintaining its clients' satisfaction every year. With a fully staffed department to assist in annual filings to the Secretary of State and providing meeting minutes every year you will never need to worry about these documents. This is why NCH, Inc. is the fastest growing resident agent today.

FULL-SERVICE COMPANY

You will be aware of the NCH, Inc. difference from the first time you speak with our corporate consultants. We realize that one size can't possibly fit everyone, so we work with you to custom fit a program to suite your specific needs. Services needed to legitimize your corporation, assist in raising capital, reviewing tax rates, and return business makes our company what it is today.

CHAPTER 11
TOTAL TAXATION

PAYING AND FILING INCOME TAXES

The federal income tax is a pay-as-you-go tax. A corporation generally must make estimated tax payments as it earns or receives income during its tax year. After the end of the year, the corporation must file an income tax return. This section will help you determine when and how to pay and file corporate income taxes.

ESTIMATED TAX

Generally, a corporation must make installment payments of estimated tax if it expects its estimated tax (income tax minus credits) to be $500 or more. If the corporation does not pay the installments when they are due, it may be subject to an underpayment penalty. This section will explain how to avoid this penalty.

When to pay estimated tax. Installment payments of estimated tax are due by the 15th day of the 4th, 6th, 9th, and 12th months of the corporation's tax year.

Example 1. Your corporation's tax year ends December 31. Installment payments of estimated tax are due on April 15, June 15, September 15, and December 15.

Example 2. Your corporation's tax year ends June 30. Installment payments of estimated tax are due on October 15, December 15, March 15, and June 15.

If any due date falls on a Saturday, Sunday, or legal holiday, the installment is due on the next regular business day.

How to figure each required installment. Use **Form 1120-W** as a worksheet to figure each required installment of estimated tax. You will generally use one of the following two methods to figure each required installment. You should use the method that requires the smallest installment payments.

Note: In these discussions, "return" generally refers to the corporation's original return. However, an amended return is considered the original return if the amended return is filed by the due date (including extensions) of the original return.

Method 1. Each required installment is 25% of the income tax the corporation will show on its return for the current year.

Method 2. Each required installment is 25% of the income tax shown on the corporation's return for the previous year.

To use Method 2:

1. The corporation must have filed a return for the previous year,

2. The return must have been for a full 12 months, and

3. The return must have shown a positive tax liability (not zero).

Also, if the corporation is a large corporation, it can use Method 2 to figure only the first installment.

A large corporation is one with at least $1 million of modified taxable income in any of the last three years. Modified taxable income is taxable income figured without net operating loss or capital loss carry backs or carryovers.

Other methods. If a corporation's income is expected to vary during the year because, for example, its business is seasonal, it may be able to lower the amount of one or more required installments by using one or both of the following methods.

1. The annualized income installment method.

2. The adjusted seasonal installment method.

Use Schedule A of Form 1120-W to see if using one or both of these methods will lower the amount of one or more required installments.

Refiguring required installments. If after the corporation figures and deposits estimated tax it finds that its tax liability for the year will be much more or less than originally estimated, it may have to refigure its required installments. If earlier installments were underpaid, the corporation may owe an underpayment penalty.

An immediate catch up payment should be made to reduce the amount of any penalty resulting from the underpayment of any earlier installments, whether caused by a change in an estimate, not making a deposit, or a mistake.

Underpayment penalty. If the corporation does not pay a required installment of estimated tax by its due date, it may be subject to a penalty. The penalty is figured separately for each installment due date. The corporation may owe a penalty for an earlier due date, even if it paid enough tax later to make up the underpayment. This is true even if the corporation is due a refund when its return is filed.

Form 2220. Use Form 2220 to determine if a corporation is subject to the penalty for underpayment of estimated tax and, if so, the amount of the penalty.

If the corporation is charged a penalty, the amount of the penalty depends on the following three factors.

1. The amount of the underpayment.

2. The period during which the underpayment was due and unpaid.

3. An interest rate for underpayments that is published quarterly by the IRS in the Internal Revenue Bulletin.

A corporation generally does not have to file Form 2220 with its income tax return because the IRS will figure any penalty and bill the corporation. However, even if the corporation does not owe a penalty, complete and attach the form to the corporation's tax return if any of the following apply.

1. The annualized income installment method was used to figure any required installment.

2. The adjusted seasonal installment method was used to figure any required installment.

3. The corporation is a large corporation and Method 2 was used to figure its first required installment.

How to pay estimated tax. Unless you volunteer or are required to make electronic deposits, you should mail or deliver your payment with a completed **Form 8109** to an authorized financial institution or to the Federal Reserve Bank for your area.

INCOME TAX RETURNS

This section will help you determine when and how to report a corporation's income tax.

Who must file. Unless exempt under section 501 of the Internal Revenue Code, all domestic corporations (including corporations in bankruptcy) must file an income tax return whether or not they have taxable income.

What form to file. A corporation must generally file **Form 1120** to report its income, gains, losses, deductions, credits, and to figure its income tax liability. However, a corporation may file **Form 1120-A** if its gross receipts, total income, and total assets are each under $500,000 and it meets certain other requirements. Also, certain organizations must file special returns. For more information, see the instructions for Forms 1120 and 1120-A.

When to file. Generally, a corporation must file its income tax return by the 15th day of the 3rd month after the end of its tax year. A new corporation filing a short-period return must generally file by the 15th day of the 3rd month after the short period ends. A corporation that has dissolved must generally file by the 15th day of the 3rd month after the date it dissolved.

> *Example 1.* A corporation's tax year ends December 31. It must file its income tax return by March 15th.

> *Example 2.* A corporation's tax year ends June 30. It must file its income tax return by September 15th.

If the due date falls on a Saturday, Sunday, or legal holiday, the corporation may file on the next business day.

Extension of time to file. File **Form 7004** to request a 6-month extension of time to file a corporation income tax return. The IRS will grant the extension if you complete the form properly, file it, and pay any balance due by the due date for the return for which the extension applies.

Form 7004 does not extend the time for paying the tax due on the return. Interest will be charged on any part of the final tax due not shown as a balance due on Form 7004. The interest is figured from the original due date of the return to the date of payment.

For more information, see the instructions for Form 7004.

Penalty for late filing of return. A corporation that does not file its tax return by the due date, including extensions, may be penalized 5% of the unpaid tax for each month or part of a month the return is late, up to a maximum of 25% of the unpaid tax. If the corporation is charged a penalty for late payment of tax (discussed next) for the same period of time, this penalty is reduced by the amount of that penalty. The minimum penalty for a return that is over 60 days late is the smaller of the tax due or $100. The penalty will not be imposed if the corporation can show that the failure to file on time was due to a reasonable cause. Corporations that file late must attach a statement explaining the reasonable cause.

Penalty for late payment of tax. A corporation that does not pay the tax when due may be penalized 1/2 of 1% of the unpaid tax for each month or part of a month the tax is not paid, up to a maximum of 25% of the unpaid tax. The penalty will not be imposed if the corporation can show that the failure to pay on time was due to a reasonable cause. However, this penalty does not apply to late payments of required installments of estimated tax.

Trust fund recovery penalty. If income, social security, and Medicare taxes that a corporation must withhold from employee wages are not withheld or are not deposited or paid to the United States Treasury, the trust fund recovery penalty may apply. The penalty is the full amount of the unpaid trust fund tax. This penalty may apply to you if these unpaid taxes cannot be immediately collected from the business.

The trust fund recovery penalty may be imposed on all persons who are determined by the IRS to be responsible for collecting, accounting for, and paying over these taxes, and who acted willfully in not doing so.

A responsible person can be an officer or employee of a corporation, an accountant, or a volunteer director/trustee. A responsible person also may include one who signs checks for the corporation or otherwise has authority to cause the spending of business funds.

Willfully means voluntarily, consciously, and intentionally. A responsible person acts willfully if the person knows the required actions are not taking place.

TAX DEDUCTIONS

In managing an active corporation, it is important to be familiar with all the aspects of how a corporation works. Part of those management responsibilities is being familiar with business expenses. Understanding expenses that are deductible and which are not is important. By familiarizing yourself with all legal business expenses, you can dramatically reduce your corporate taxes and get more personal tax-free perks. Rules on income and deductions that apply to individuals also apply, for the most part, to corporations. However, some of the following special provisions apply only to corporations.

SELECTED BUSINESS EXPENSES

Car Mileage. 31.5 cents per mile is the current rate that a business can reimburse an individual for using his car for business purposes. This is not considered income to the individual. (Note: an alternative to this is to rent a car to a corporation. This is a way of drawing funds out of a corporation without employee taxes or self-employment taxes being paid on rental income.)

Automobile Lease Program. This is for vehicles leased by the corporation.

Meals and Lodging. Generally you can deduct the costs of these as long as the expense is an ordinary and necessary business expense. Regular business meals are now only fifty percent deductible.

Education Expenses. A business can fully deduct educational expenses for employees as long as the education is job related.

Employee Health Insurance.

Employee Dental Insurance.

State Income Tax. If a corporation has to pay state income tax, this is a deductible item. However, if the business is a Nevada corporation, there is no state income tax.

Child Care. You can pay up to $5,000 annually for an employee's childcare without considering it income to the employee. (This is not an option for those individuals that are contractors of a corporation.)

Below-Market Loans. A below-market loan is a loan on which no interest is charged or on which interest is charged at a rate below the applicable federal rate. A below-market loan generally is treated as an arm's-length transaction in which the borrower is treated as having received:

• A loan in exchange for a note that requires payment of interest at the applicable federal rate, and

• An additional payment.

Treat the additional payment as a gift, dividend, contribution to capital, payment of compensation, or other payment, depending on the substance of the transaction.

Capital Losses. A corporation can deduct capital losses only up to the amount of its capital gains. In other words, if a corporation has an excess capital loss, it cannot deduct the loss in the current tax year. It carries the loss to other tax years and deducts it from capital gains that occur in those years.

First, carry a net capital loss back three years. Deduct it from any total net capital gain that occurred in that year. If you do not deduct the full loss, carry it forward one year (two years back) and then one more year (one year back). If any loss remains, carry it over to future tax years, one year at a time, for up to five years. When you carry a net capital loss to another tax year, treat it as a short-term loss. It does not retain its original identity as long term or short term.

Example. In 1999, a calendar year corporation has a net short-term capital gain of $3,000 and a net long-term capital loss of $9,000. The short-term gain offsets some of the long-term loss, leaving a net capital loss of $6,000. It treats this $6,000 as a short-term loss when carried back or forward.

The corporation carries the $6,000 short-term loss back three years to 1996. In 1996, the corporation had a net short-term capital gain of $8,000 and a net long-term capital gain of $5,000. It subtracts the $6,000 short-term loss from 1999 first from the net short-term gain. This results in a net capital gain for 1996 of $7,000. This consists of a net short-term capital gain of $2,000 ($8,000 - $6,000) and a net long-term capital gain of $5,000.

"S" corporation status. A corporation may not carry a capital loss from, or to, a year for which it is an S corporation.

Rules for carryover and carry back. When carrying a capital loss from one year to another, the following rules apply.

- When figuring this year's net capital loss, you cannot use any capital loss carried from another year. In other words, you may carry capital losses only to years that would otherwise have a total net capital gain.

- If you carry capital losses from two or more years to the same year, deduct the loss from the earliest year first. When you fully deduct that loss, deduct the loss from the next earliest year, and so on.

- You cannot use a capital loss carried from another year to produce or increase a net operating loss in the year to which you carry it.

When you carry back a capital loss to an earlier tax year, refigure your tax for that year. If your corrected tax is less than you originally owed, you may apply for a refund.

Charitable Contributions. A corporation can claim a limited deduction for any charitable contributions made in cash or other property. The contribution is deductible if made to or for the use of a qualified organization.

You cannot take a deduction if any of the net earnings of an organization receiving contributions benefit any private shareholder or individual.

You can ask any organization whether it is a qualified organization, and most will be able to tell you. Or you can check IRS Publication 78, *Cumulative List of Organizations,* which lists most qualified organizations. You may find Publication 78 in your local library's reference section.

OTHER DEDUCTIONS ALLOWED FOR A CORPORATION BUT NOT AN INDIVIDUAL ARE:

1. Half of FICA at 7.65%.
2. The 70% Dividend Exclusion Rule –allowing a corporation to deduct 70% of any dividends it earns.
3. Meals & lodging provided for the convenience of the employer.
4. Travel, lodging and meals associated with the Directors or Officers and Shareholders meetings.
5. Group insurance is fully deductible for owners if they are also employees.
6. All ordinary business expenses may be deducted for traders of commodities or stocks.
7. Employee achievement awards up to $400 value.
8. Catered meals are allowed to be paid for.
9. Fringe benefits for the officers, directors and shareholders.
10. Real estate losses can offset active corporate income.

START UP BUSINESS DEDUCTIONS

When you go into business, treat all costs you incur to get your business started as capital expenses. Capital expenses are part of your basis in the business. Generally, you recover costs for particular assets through depreciation deductions. However, you generally cannot recover other costs until you sell the business or otherwise go out of business.

You can choose to amortize certain costs for setting up your business. The cost must qualify as one of the following.

- A business start-up cost.

- An organizational cost.

Start-up costs are costs for creating an active trade or business or investigating the creation or acquisition of an active trade or business. Start-up costs include any amounts paid or incurred in connection with any activity engaged in for profit and for the production of income before the trade or business begins, in anticipation of the activity becoming an active trade or business.

A start-up cost is amortizable if it meets both of the following tests.

- It is a cost you could deduct if you paid or incurred it to operate an existing active trade or business (in the same field).

- It is a cost you pay or incur before the day your active trade or business begins.

Start-up costs can include costs for the following items.

- A survey of potential markets.

- An analysis of available facilities, labor, supplies, etc.

- Advertisements for the opening of the business.

- Salaries and wages for employees who are being trained, and their instructors.

- Travel and other necessary costs for securing prospective distributors, suppliers, or customers.

- Salaries and fees for executives and consultants, or for other professional services.

Start-up costs do not include deductible interest, taxes, or research and experimental costs.

Amortizable start-up costs for purchasing an active trade or business include only costs incurred in the course of a general search for or preliminary investigation of the business. Investigative costs are the costs that help you decide whether to purchase the business and which business to purchase. Costs you incur in the attempt to purchase a specific business are capital expenses and you cannot amortize them.

If you completely dispose of your business before the end of the amortization period, you can deduct any remaining deferred start-up costs. However, you can only deduct these deferred start-up costs to the extent they qualify as a loss from a business.

You can amortize an organizational cost only if it meets all of the following tests.

- It is for the creation of the corporation.
- It is chargeable to a capital account.
- You could amortize the cost over the life of the corporation, if the corporation had a fixed life.

You must have incurred the cost before the end of the first tax year in which the corporation was in business. A corporation using the cash method of accounting can amortize organizational costs incurred within the first tax year, even if it does not pay them in that year.

The following are examples of organizational costs.

- Costs of temporary directors.
- The cost of organizational meetings.
- State incorporation fees.
- Accounting services for setting up the corporation.
- The cost of legal services (such as drafting the charter, bylaws, terms of the original stock certificates, and minutes of organizational meetings).

Costs you cannot amortize. The following costs are not organizational costs. You must capitalize them.

- Costs for issuing and selling stock or securities, such as commissions, professional fees, and printing costs.
- Costs associated with the transfer of assets to the corporation.

How to amortize. You deduct start-up and organizational costs in equal amounts over a period of 60 months or more. You can choose a period for start-up costs that is different from the period you choose for organizational costs, as long as both are 60 months or more. Once you choose an amortization period, you cannot change it.

To figure your deduction, divide your total start-up or organizational costs by the months in the amortization period. The result is the amount you can deduct each month.

The amortization period starts with the month you begin business operations.

Shareholder costs. Only your corporation can choose to amortize its start-up or organizational costs. A shareholder cannot make this choice. You, as a shareholder, cannot amortize any costs you incur in setting up your corporation. The corporation can amortize these costs.

Depending on which accounting method the corporation is using the tax deduction will be treated differently.

Cash method corporation. A corporation using the cash method of accounting can deduct contributions only in the tax year paid.

Accrual method corporation. A corporation using an accrual method of accounting can choose to deduct unpaid contributions for the tax year the board of directors authorizes them if it pays them within two and a half months after the close of that tax year. Make the choice by reporting the contribution on the corporation's return for the tax year. A copy of the resolution authorizing the contribution and a declaration stating that the board of directors adopted the resolution during the tax year must accompany the return. An officer authorized to sign the return must sign the declaration under penalties of perjury.

A corporation cannot deduct as charitable contributions for a tax year more than 10% of its taxable income. Figure taxable income for this purpose without the following.

A corporation that uses an accrual method of accounting cannot deduct business expenses and interest owed to a related person who uses the cash method of accounting until the corporation makes the payment and the corresponding amount is includible in the related person's gross income. Determine the relationship, for this rule, as of the end of the tax year for which the expense or interest would otherwise be deductible. If a deduction is denied under this rule, the rule will continue to apply even if the corporation's relationship with the person ends before the expense or interest is includible in the gross income of that person. These rules also deny the deduction of losses on the sale or exchange of property between related persons.

Related persons. For purposes of this rule, the following persons are related to a corporation.

1. Another corporation that is a member of the same controlled group.

2. An individual who owns, directly or indirectly, more than 50% of the value of the outstanding stock of the corporation.

3. A trust fiduciary when the trust or the grantor of the trust owns, directly or indirectly, more than 50% in value of the outstanding stock of the corporation.

4. An S corporation if the same persons own more than 50% in value of the outstanding stock of each corporation.

5. A partnership if the same persons own more than 50% in value of the outstanding stock of the corporation and more than 50% of the capital or profits interest in the partnership.

6. Any employee-owner if the corporation is a personal service corporation (defined later), regardless of the amount of stock owned by the employee-owner.

Ownership of stock. To determine whether an individual directly or indirectly owns any of the outstanding stock of a corporation, the following rules apply.

1. Stock owned, directly or indirectly, by or for a corporation, partnership, estate, or trust is treated as being owned proportionately by or for its shareholders, partners, or beneficiaries.

2. An individual is treated as owning the stock owned, directly or indirectly, by or for his or her family. Family includes only brothers and sisters (including half brothers and half sisters), a spouse, ancestors, and lineal descendants.

3. Any individual owning (other than by applying rule (2)) any stock in a corporation is treated as owning the stock owned directly or indirectly by that individual's partner.

To apply rule (1), (2), or (3), stock constructively owned by a person under rule (1) is treated as actually owned by that person. But stock constructively owned by an individual under rule (2) or (3) is not treated as actually owned by the individual for applying either rule (2) or (3) to make another person the constructive owner of that stock.

The following tax charts and information is taken from ALL STATES TAX HANDBOOK, 2000 EDITION by RESEARCH INSTITUTE OF AMERICA.

Forty-four states and the District of Columbia allow their courts to be used to collect unpaid taxes of other states. In each case, the right to use the courts of the particular state depends upon reciprocity—that is, the taxing state must extend like courtesy in its courts. It's not necessary to obtain a judgment in the taxing state before filing suit in any of these jurisdictions.

Alabama, Alaska, Arizona, Arkansas, California, Colorado, Connecticut, Delaware, District of Columbia, Georgia, Hawaii, Idaho, Illinois, Indiana, Iowa, Kansas, Kentucky, Louisiana, Maine, Maryland, Massachusetts, Michigan, Minnesota, Mississippi, Missouri, Nebraska, New Hampshire, New Jersey, New York, North Carolina, North Dakota, Ohio, Oklahoma, Oregon, Pennsylvania, Rhode Island, South Carolina, South Dakota, Tennessee, Texas, (sales use only), Vermont, Virginia, Washington, West Virginia, Wisconsin.

Tax Chart of Some of the Taxes Levied in Every State

	Capital Values Franchise	Corporation Income	Individual Income	Stock Transfer	Inheritance
Alabama	Yes	5%	2% 1st $500 4% next $2,500 5% over $3,000	Yes	No
Alaska	No	1%, 1st $10M 2% next $10M 3% next $10M 4% next $10M 5% next $10M 6% next $10M 7% next $10M 8% next $10M 9% next $10M 9.4% over $90M	No Personal Income Tax	No	No
Arizona	No	8% Min. $50	2.87% 1st $10,000 3.2% next $15,000 3.74% next 25,000 4.72% next 100,000 5.04% on over $150,000	No	No

TAX CHART OF SOME OF THE TAXES
LEVIED IN EVERY STATE

	Capital Values Franchise	Corporation Income	Individual Income	Stock Transfer	Inheritance
Arkansas	Yes	1% 1st $3M 2% 2nd $3M 3% next $5M 5% next $14M 6% next $75M 6.5% over $100,000	1% 1st $3,099 2.5% next $3,000 3.5% next $3,100 4.5% next $6,100 6% next $10,100 7% on $25,400 & over	No	No
California	No	8.84%	1% 1st $10,528 2% next $14,42 4% next $14,430 6% next $15,290 8% next $14,422 9.3% over $69,096	No	No
Colorado	No	4.75%	4.75%	No	No
Connecticut	Yes	8.5%	3% 1st $10,000 4.5% balance	No	Yes (40)
Delaware	Yes (28)	8.7%	No tax 1st $2,000 2.6% next $3,000 4.3% next $5,000 5.2% next $10,000 5.6% next $5,000 5.95% next $35,000 6.4% over $60,000	No	(38)
District of Columbia	No	9.5% + 5% surtax Minimum $100	6% 1st $10,000 8% 2nd $10,000 9.5% on over $20,000 (8)	No	No
Florida	No	5.5%	None	Yes	No
Georgia	Yes	6%	1% 1st $750 2% next $1,500 3% next $1,500 4% next $1,500 5% next $1,750 6% over $7,000	No	No

TAX CHART OF SOME OF THE TAXES LEVIED IN EVERY STATE

	Capital Values Franchise	Corporation Income	Individual Income	Stock Transfer	Inheritance
Hawaii	No	4.4% 1st $25M 5.4% next $75M 6.4% over $100M	1.6% 1st $4,000 3.9% next $4,000 6.8% next $8,000 7.2% next $8,000 7.5% next $8,000 7.8% next $8,000 8.2% next $20,000 8.5% next $20,000 8.75% over $80,000	No	No
Idaho	Yes	8%	2% 1st $1,000 4% 2nd $1,000 4.5% 3rd $1,000 5.5% 4th $1,000 6.5% 5th $1,000 7.5% next $2,500 7.8% next $12,500 8.2% over $20,000; Plus $10 excise	No	No
Illinois	Yes	4.8%	3%	No	No
Indiana	No	3.4%	3.4%	No	Yes
Iowa	No	6% 1st $25M 8% next $75M 10% next $150M 12% over $250M	.36% 1st $1,148 .72% next $1,148 2.43% next $2,296 4.5% next $5,740 6.12% next $6,890 6.48% next $5,740 6.8% next $11,480 7.92% next 17,220 8.98% over $51,660	No	Yes
Kansas	Yes	4% + 3.35% surtax on over $50M	3.5% 1st $30,000 6.25% next 30,000 6.45% on balance	No	Yes (42)
Kentucky	Yes	4% on 1st $25M 5% on 2nd $25M 6% on next $50M 7% on next $150M 8.25% over $250M	2% 1st $3,000 3% 4th $1,000 4% 5th $1,000 5% next $3,000 6% over $8,000	No	Yes

TAX CHART OF SOME OF THE TAXES
LEVIED IN EVERY STATE

	Capital Values Franchise	Corporation Income	Individual Income	Stock Transfer	Inheritance
Louisiana	Yes	4% on 1st $25M 5% on 2nd $25M 6% on next $50M 7% on next $100M 8% over $200M	2% 1st $10,000 4% next $40,000 6% over $50,000	No	Yes
Maine	No	3.5% on 1st $25M 7.93%, next $50M 8.33% next $175M 8.93% over $250M`	2% 1st $2,750 4.5% next $4,100 7% next $8,250 8.5% over $16,500	No	No
Maryland	No	7%	2% 1st $1,000 3% 2nd $1,000 4% 3rd $1,000 4.85% over $3,000	No	Yes
Massachusets	Yes	Excise: $2.60 per $M on tangible values or net worth + 9.5% (incl. 14% surtax) of net income; $456 min.	5.95% interest, dividends; 12% short-term capital gains; 5.95% all other income	No	No
Michigan	No	2.2% (7)	4.4% (7)	No	No
Minnesota	No	9.8%	5.5% 1st $25,220 7.25% next 74,980 8% over $100,200	No	No
Mississippi	Yes	3% 1st $5,000 4% next $5,000 5% over $10,000	3% 1st $5,000 4% next $5,000 5% over $10,000	No	No
Missouri	Yes	6.25%	1.5% 1st $1,000 2% next $1,000 2.5% next $1,000 3% next $1,000 3.5% next $1,000 4% next $1,000 4.5% next $1,000 5% next $1,000 5.5% next $1,000 6% over $9,000	No	No

TAX CHART OF SOME OF THE TAXES LEVIED IN EVERY STATE

	Capital Values Franchise	Corporation Income	Individual Income	Stock Transfer	Inheritance
Montana	No	6.75% Min. $50	1st $2,000, 2% next $2,000, 3% (- $20 tax) next $4,000, 4% (- $60 tax) next $4,100, 5% (- $140 tax) next $4,000, 6% (-$261 tax) next $4,000, 7% (-$422 tax) next $8,100, 8% (- $623 tax) next $12,000, 9% (- $905 tax) next $30,200, 10% (-$1,307 tax) over $70,400, 11% (-$2,011 tax)	No	Yes
Nebraska	Yes	5.58% 1st $50M 7.81% over $50M	2.51% 1st $2,400 3.49% next 14,600 5.01% next $9,500 6.68% over $26,500	No	Yes
Nevada	No	No tax	None	No	No
New Hampshire	No	8% (13)	5% (9)	No	Yes
New Jersey	No	9%	1.4% 1st $20,000 1.75%, on next $30,000 2.45% next 20,000 3.5% next $10,000 5.525% next $70,000 6.37% over 150,000	No	Yes (16)
New Mexico	No	4.8% on 1st $500M 6.4% on 2nd $500M 7.6% on over $1 million	1.7% 1st $5,500 3.2% next $5,500 4.7% next $5,000 6% next $10,000 7.1% next $16,000 7.9% next $23,000 8.2% over $65,000	No	No
New York	Yes	8.5%	4% 1st $8,000 4.5% next $3,000 5.25% next $2,000 5.9% next $7,000 6.85% over $20,000	Yes (32)	No

TAX CHART OF SOME OF THE TAXES
LEVIED IN EVERY STATE

	Capital Values Franchise	Corporation Income	Individual Income	Stock Transfer	Inheritance
North Carolina	Yes	7%	6% on 1st $12,750 7% on next $47,250 7.75% over $60,000	No	(41)
North Dakota	No	3% on 1st $3,000 4.5% next $5,000 6% next $12,000 7.5% next $10,000 9% next $20,000 10.5% over $50,000	2.67% on 1st $3000 4% next $2,000 5.33% next $3,000 6.67% next $7,000 8% next $10,000 9.33% next $10,000 10.67% next $15,000 12% over $50,000	No	No
Ohio	Yes	5.1% on 1st $50,000 plus 8.5% on over $50,000, Min. $50	0.743% 1st $5,000 1.486% next $5,000 2.972% next $5,000 3.715% next $5,000 4.457% next $20,000 5.201% next $40,000 5.943% next $20,000 6.9% next $100,000 7.5% over $200,000	No	No
Oklahoma	Yes	6%	0.5% 1st $1000 1% next $1,500 2% next $1,250 3% next $1,150 4% next $1,300 5% next $1,500 6% next $2,300 6.75% over $10,000	No	No
Oregon	No	6.6%, Min. $10	5% 1st $2,350 7% next $3,500 9% over $5,850	No	No
Pennsylvania	Yes	9.99%	2.8%	No	Yes
Rhode Island	Yes	9%. Min $250	26.5% on Fed Tax	No	No

TAX CHART OF SOME OF THE TAXES LEVIED IN EVERY STATE

	Capital Values Franchise	Corporation Income	Individual Income	Stock Transfer	Inheritance
South Carolina	Yes	5%	1st $2,340, 2.5% next $2,340, 3% (- $11 tax) next $2,340, 4% (-$58 tax) next $2,340, 5% (-$128 tax) next $2,340, 6% (-$222 tax) on over $11,700, 7% (-$339 tax)	No	No
South Dakota	No	No broad based income tax (23)	None	No	Yes
Tennessee	Yes	6%	6% on income from stock–bonds (9)	No	Yes
Texas	Yes	No broad based income tax, but has a franchise tax	None	No	Yes
Utah	No	5%, Min $1,00	2.3% 1st $750 3.3% next $750 4.2% next $750 5.2% next $750 6% next $750 7% on over $3,750	No	No
Vermont	No	7% on 1st $10,000 8.1% on next $15,000 9.2% next $225,000 9.75% over $250,000	25% of Federal Income Tax	No	No
Virginia	No	6%	2% 1st $3,000 3% next $2,000 5% next $12,000 5.75% over $17,000	No	No
Washington	No	No income tax– But a Buisness & Occupation Tax is levied	None	No	No
West Virginia	Yes	9%	3% 1st $10,000 4% next $15,000 6% next $20,000 6.5% over $60,000	No	No

TAX CHART OF SOME OF THE TAXES
LEVIED IN EVERY STATE

	Capital Values Franchise	Corporation Income	Individual Income	Stock Transfer	Inheritance
Wisconsin	No	7.9%	4.77% 1ˢᵗ $10,160 6.37% next $10,160 6.77% over $20,320	No	No
Wyoming	Yes	No broad based income tax	None	No	No

7   Mich. – "Single Business Tax" applies to corporations and individuals. Effective 1-1-99, single business tax is being phased out at 0.1% per year if statutory requirements are met.

8   D.C. – Net income tax is also imposed on unincorporated business.

9   N.H. & Tenn. – Tax is on income from intangibles only.

13   N.H. Business profits tax is on corporations, partnerships, individuals and other organizations operated for profit. Business enterprise tax on compensation, interest, and dividends is also imposed.

16   N.J. Inheritance tax is imposed on persons other than the surviving spouse and direct lineal ascendants or descendants.

23   S.D. Only financial institutions pay tax.

28   Del. No tax on foreign corporations.

38   Del. Inheritance tax was repealed effective for estates of persons dying after 12-31-98.

40   Conn. Inheritance tax is repealed effective for estates of persons dying after 12-31-2004.

41   N.C. Inheritance tax was repealed effective for estates of persons dying after 12-31-98.

42   Kan. Inheritance tax was repealed effective for estates of persons dying after 6-30-98.

Fees payable on corporate organization or qualification. The fees payable to a state on corporate organization or qualification to do business there are charted below. In many states, newly organized domestic corporations and qualifying foreign corporations must pay the state's franchise or capital stock tax when organizing, qualifying, or domesticating—the rates and bases of state franchise taxes are in the section below.

CORPORATE ORGANIZATION AND ENTRANCE FEES INITIAL TAXES

STATE	MEASURE AND RATE OF TAX
Alabama	Organization fee – domestic: filing fee $75. Permit fee $10 if paid capital stock less than $25,000; $20 if over $25,000 but less than $50,000; $30 if over $50,000 but less than $100,000; $50 if over $100,000 but less than $150,000; $100 if over $150,000. Franchise tax listed below. Entrance fee – foreign; Filing fee $175. Permit fee $5 if capital employed instate is less than $1,000; $10 if over $1,000 but less than $10,000; $20 if over $10,000 but less than $25,000; $50 if over $25,000 but less than $50,000; $100 if over $50,000; plus admission tax of 25% of 1st $100 of capital employed instate, 5% of next $900, and 0.1% of amount over $1,000. Franchise tax listed below. Annual Report: For domestic and foreign, $10 fee plus permit fee plus franchise tax listed below.
Alaska	Organization & entrance fees – domestic and foreign: $150 Biennial report & license fee: $100 for domestic; $200 foreign.
Arizona	Organization & entrance fees – domestic, $60; foreign, $175 Annual report & registration fee: $45 for domestic and foreign.
Arkansas	Organization fee – domestic: $50 Entrance fee – foreign: $300 Franchise Tax listed below
California	Initial Taxes – domestic: Stock corporations, $100 plus min franchise tax of $800. If incorporated after 1/1/00 no minimum franchise tax for first two years. Biennial statement $20. Entrance Fee – Foreign: Stock corporations, $100 plus min franchise tax of $800. If incorporated after 1/1/00 no minimum franchise tax for first two years. Biennial statement $20.
Colorado	Organization fees – domestic: Filing articles of incorporation; $50 Entrance Fees – foreign; Application for certificate of authority $75 Corporate (biennial) report: Domestic $25; foreign $100

STATE	MEASURE AND RATE OF TAX
Connecticut	Initial Taxes – domestic: $.01 authorized share on 1ˢᵗ 10,000 shares; next 90,000 $.005 next 900,000, $.0025 over 1,000,000 shares, $.0025 min. $150. $50 filing fee. Entrance Fee – foreign: $225 annual license fee. $50 filing fee. Annual report: Domestic & foreign: $75 annual filing fee. For foreign, add $225 annual license fee.
Delaware	Initial tax – domestic: Par value $.02 per $100 of authorized capital stock for 1ˢᵗ $2,000,000; $.01 per $100 on next $18,000,000; $.04 per $100 over $20,000,000. No-par: $.01 per share for 1ˢᵗ 20,000 shares: $.05 per share on next 1,800,000; $.04 per share over 2,000,000 shares. Min. $15. $25 filing fee. Entrance fee – foreign : $80 plus $50 filing fee. Annual Report: Domestic, $20 plus franchise tax listed below; foreign, $50.
District of Columbia	Organization fee – domestic: Authorized shares: $.02 per share on first 10,000: $.01 next 40,000; $.005 over 50,000 min. fee $20. $100 filing fee. Entrance fee – foreign: Flat fee of $150 2-yr. – report domestic and foreign, $200 fee
Florida	Organization & entrance filing fees – Domestic and foreign: $123.75 Annual Report: Domestic – foreign $150
Georgia	Organization & entrance fees: Domestic $60; foreign $170 Annual registration: Domestic and foreign, $15
Hawaii	Organization fee – domestic $100 Entrance fee – foreign. Flat fee of $100. Also license fee of $100. Annual Report – domestic and foreign $25
Idaho	Organization and entrance fees – domestic and foreign: $100 if form typed, $120 if not typed or if with attachments. Annual report: Domestic and foreign – no fee
Illinois	Initial taxes: domestic: $75 plus franchise tax listed below Entrance fees – foreign: $75 plus franchise tax listed below Annual report: Domestic and foreign, $25 plus franchise fee listed below
Indiana	Organization and entrance fees: $90 for domestic and foreign. Biennial report: Domestic and foreign, $30
Iowa	Organization fees – domestic: $50 for certificate of incorporation. Entrance fees – foreign: Filing certificate of authority; $100 Biennial report $60
Kansas	Initial taxes – domestic: Application and recording fee: $75 Entrance Fee – foreign: $95 fee. Ltd. Partnership $150 filing fee: business trust $50. Annual report required

STATE	MEASURE AND RATE OF TAX
Kentucky	Organization fees – domestic: Par and no value stock - $.01 per share up to 20,000; $.005 on next 180,000 shares; $.0025 per share over 200,000. Min $10. Plus $90 incorporation fee. Plus $8 recording fee to county court clerk. Entrance fees – foreign. Filing certificate of authority, $90. Plus $8 recording fee to county court clerk. Annual report: Domestic and foreign, $15
Louisiana	Initial & entrance fees: Domestic, $60; foreign, $100. Annual report: domestic and foreign, $25.
Maine	Organization tax – domestic: Par value: Up to $2,000,000, $30 per $100M; next $18,000,000, $150 per million; $3,300 plus $70 per million over $20,000,000. No par – 1st 20,000 shares, $.01 per share; next 19,980,000, $.005; over 2 million, $.0025. Min. tax $30. Plus $75 organization tax. Entrance Fee – foreign; $180. Annual report: Domestic and foreign, $60
Maryland	Organization tax – domestic: Based on authorized capital stock – 1st $100M, $20; next $900 M, $20 plus $1 per $5M; next $1 million, $200 plus $10 per $100M; next $3 million, $300 plus $15 per $500M; over $5 million, $390 plus $20 per added $1 million. No par value at $20 per share. Min tax $20. Add $20 recording fee. Domestic without capital stock, savings and loan assns., credit unions, and cooperative assn. Pay $20 fee. Entrance fee – foreign: $50 flat qualification fee. Annual report: Domestic and foreign, $100
Massachusettes	Organization fees – domestic: On authorized stock – 1/10% of par value. Min. $200 Entrance fee – foreign: Fee for filing initial certificate with State Secretary, $300. Annual Report: Domestic and foreign $85
Michigan	Organization and admission (franchise) fee domestic and foreign: $50 for 1st 60,000 authorized shares and $30 per added 20,000 authorized shares, up to max. of $5,000 for 1st 10 million shares and $200,000 for the rest. Add $10 filing fee. Annual report: Domestic and foreign. $15
Minnesota	Organization tax- domestic: $100 flat incorporation fee plus $35 filing fee. Annual report due; no fee generally. Entrance fee – foreign: initial License (qualification) fee is $150 plus $50 filing fee. Annual report and license fee. $20 per $100,000 of Minn. Net taxable income ($40 min.) Plus $20 annual report fee.
Mississippi	Organization and entrance fees – domestic and foreign; Fees for filing incorporation articles; $50; application for certificate of authority; $500 1st yr. Info statement – domestic and foreign, pay franchise tax as listed below Annual report: Domestic and foreign $25

STATE	MEASURE AND RATE OF TAX
Missouri	Organization tax – domestic: $50 plus $5 per added $10,000 over $30,000 of capital stock (no par shares valued at $1 each) Add $8 filing fee. Entrance fee – foreign $150 plus added $5 fee. Annual registration fee: $40
Montana	Organization fee – domestic: If 50,000 or fewer shares authorized, $50 fee; 50,000 – 100,000, $100; 100,000 – 250,000, $250; 250,000 – 500,000, $400; 500,000 – 1,000,000, $600; Over 1 million, $1,000. Min. fee $50. Add $20 filing Fee Entrance fee – foreign: $100. Add $20 filing fee. Annual report: Domestic and foreign, $10.
Nebraska	Organization fee – domestic and domesticated: Authorized capital stock: $10,000 or less, $60; $10,001 – 25,000, $100; $25,001-50,000, $150; $50,001 –75,000, $225; $75,001 – 100,000, $300; over $100,000, $300 plus $3 per $1,000 over $100,000. Add $5 per page recording fee. Entrance fees – foreign $130, plus $5 per page recording fee.
Nevada	Organization fee – domestic: Based on authorized capital stock up to $25,000, $125; $75,000, $175; $200,000, $225; $500,000, $325; $1,000,000, $425; $425 plus $225 per $500,000 over $1,000,000. $25,000 max fee. Entrance Fee – foreign. Same as for Domestic. Annual Report: Domestic and foreign, $85
New Hampshire	Organization fee – domestic: $35 filing fee. Added $50 to file registration statement. Entrance fee – foreign: $35 filing fee. Added $50 to file registration statement. Annual report: Domestic and Foreign $100
New Jersey	Organization fee – domestic: $100 Entrance fee – foreign $100 Annual report: domestic and foreign, $40 Annual report of unauthorized foreign corporations: No tax
New Mexico	Organization & entrance fees – domestic and foreign: $1 for every 1,000 shares of total capital stock authorized; min. $100 for domestic, $200 for foreign; $1,000 max. No par stock valued at $10 per share. Biennial report: Domestic and foreign, $25
New York	Organization tax – domestic: Tax at 1/20% on par value of shares and $.05 on each no par share. Min $10 Entrance Fee – domestic: $125, foreign $225 License fee – foreign: Capital stock employed in state 1/20% of par value and $.05 per share on no-par stock. Min. $10. Maintenance fee – foreign: $300 generally. Biennial report – domestic and foreign, $9.
North Carolina	Initial taxes – domestic $125 Entrance fee – foreign $250 Annual report – domestic and foreign: $20

STATE	MEASURE AND RATE OF TAX
North Dakota	Organization fee – domestic: $50 on 1st $50,000 of authorized capital stock; $10 per $10,000 stock or fraction over $50,000; min. $50 fee. No par shares valued at $1. Add $30 filing fee. Entrance fee – foreign: $85 entrance fee, plus $40 filing fee, plus same fee as for domestic but based on property gross receipts in state. Annual report: Domestic and foreign, $25
Ohio	Organization fee – domestic: Based on shares authorized (par or no-par); up to 1,000 shares, $.10 per share; next 9,000, $.05; next 40,000, $.02; next 50,000 shares, $.01; next 400,000, $.005; over 500,000 shares, $.0025 a share (plus $3,850). Min. $85 Entrance fee: foreign – $100 filing fee plus same fee per shares as domestic but times ratio of Ohio to total property and business. Annual report – domestic: report – pay income tax
Oklahoma	Organization fee – domestic: 0.1% of authorized capital stock. Min. $50. No par share valued at $50. Entrance fees – foreign: fee is 0.1% of maximum capital invested in-state during current fiscal year. Min. $300. No par share valued at $50. Annual certificate: of capital invested instate – foreign: fee of .1% of capital invested in state and upon which no fee was previously paid. Filing fee $10.
Oregon	Filing fee – domestic: $50 Entrance fee – foreign $440 Annual report – domestic corps, $30 – Foreign, $220
Pennsylvania	Initial fees: Certificate of incorporation, $100; certificate of authority, $180
Rhode Island	Organization and entrance fees – domestic and foreign; Up to 10,000 authorized shares, $.01 per share; next 90,000, $.005; over 100,000, $.0025 per share. Min. – domestic, $80; foreign $15. Plus filing fee – domestic, $70; foreign, $150. Annual report: Domestic & foreign, $50
South Carolina	Organization tax and entrance fee – domestic and foreign; $100 tax plus $10 filing fee.
South Dakota	Organization and entrance fees – domestic and foreign; Based on authorized capital stock – 1st $25,000, $90; $25 - $100,000, $110; $100 - $500,000, $130; $500 - $1,000,000, $150; over $1,000,000, $200 plus $50 per added $500,000 or portion over $1,000,000; over $5,000,000, $550 plus $40 per added $500,000. No par valued at $100 per share. Max fee $16,000. Annual report: Domestic and foreign, $25
Tennessee	Organization fee – domestic: $100 filing fee. Entrance fee – foreign; $600 filing fee Annual report: Domestic and foreign, $20 filing fee

STATE	MEASURE AND RATE OF TAX
Texas	Organization fee – domestic: Flat fee $300. Entrance fee – foreign: fee for certificate of authority $750. Annual public information report: no fee
Utah	Organization and entrance fees: domestic and foreign – $50 Annual report: Domestic and foreign, $10
Vermont	Organization Fee – domestic $75 Entrance fee – Foreign $100 Annual Report – foreign, $150; domestic $25
Virginia	Entrance fees – domestic and foreign; Authorized shares one million or less, $50 per 256,000 shares; if over one million, $2,500. Add $25 filing fee. Annual registration fees: Domestic and Foreign corporations doing business in Va. Pay: Up to 5,000 authorized shares, $50; over 5,000 , $15 per 5,000 shares or fraction; max., $850. Annual report: No fee.
Washington	Organization and entrance fees – domestic and foreign; $175 Annual report: Domestic and foreign, $50 annual license fee.
West Virginia	Initial & entrance fees – domestic and foreign: $10 filing fee plus license tax Business activity report: Domestic and foreign (no filing fee) Business registration tax: $30 for 2 yr. period.
Wisconsin	Organization fee – domestic: $.01 per authorized share; $90 min.; $10,000 max. Entrance fee – foreign: $100, plus $2 per $1,000 of capital over $60,000 expected to be employed in state. Annual report: Domestic, $25. Foreign, $50
Wyoming	Organization fee – domestic: $100 Entrance fee foreign: $100 Annual reports: Pay license tax

FEDERAL TAX CHART FOR 2000

	Taxable Income Over	Not Exceeding	Tax +	Rate of Excess	Tax on Excess of
Form 1040: Married, Filing Jointly	$ 0 $ 43,850 $105,950 $161,450 $288,350	$ 43,850 $105,950 $161,450 $288,350	$ 0 $ 6,578 $23,966 $41,171 $86,855	15% 28% 31% 36% 39.6%	$ 0 $ 43,850 $105,950 $161,450 $288,350
Form 1040: Married, Filing Separately	$ 0 $ 21,925 $ 52,975 $ 80,725 $144,175	$ 21,925 $ 52,975 $ 80,725 $144,175	$ 0 $ 3,289 $11,983 $20,586 $43,428	15% 28% 31% 36% 39.6%	$ 0 $ 21,925 $ 52,975 $ 80,725 $144,175
Form 1040: Head of Household	$ 0 $ 35,150 $ 90,800 $147,050 $288,350	$ 35,150 $ 90,800 $147,050 $288,350	$ 0 $ 5,273 $20,855 $38,292 $89,160	15% 28% 31% 36% 39.6%	$ 0 $ 35,150 $ 90,800 $147,050 $288,350
Form 1040: Single	$ 0 $ 26,250 $ 63,550 $132,600 $288,350	$ 26,250 $ 63,550 $132,600 $288,350	$ 0 $ 3,938 $14,382 $35,787 $91,857	15% 28% 31% 36% 39.6%	$ 0 $ 26,250 $ 63,550 $132,600 $288,350
Form 1120: Corporations	$ 0 $ 50,000 $ 75,000 $ 100,000 $ 335,000 $10,000,000 $15,000,000 $18,333,333	$ 50,000 $ 75,000 $ 100,000 $ 335,000 $10,000,000 $15,000,000 $18,333,333	$ 0 $ 7,500 $ 13,750 $ 22,250 $ 113,900 $3,400,000 $5,150,000 $6,416,667	15% 25% 34% 39% 34% 35% 38% 35%	$ 0 $ 50,000 $ 75,000 $ 100,000 $ 335,000 $10,000,000 $15,000,000 $18,333,333
Form 1041: Estate & Trusts	$ 0 $1,750 $4,050 $6,200 $8,450	$1,750 $4,050 $6,200 $8,450	$ 0 $ 263 $ 907 $1,573 $2,383	15% 28% 31% 36% 39.6%	$ 0 $1,750 $4,050 $6,200 $8,450

FEDERAL ESTATE TAX AND UNIFIED CREDIT FOR ESTATE AND GIFT TAXES

Taxable Income Over	Not Exceeding	Tax	Tax on Excess of
$ 0	$ 10,000	$ 0	18%
$ 10,000	$ 20,000	$ 1,800	20%
$ 20,000	$ 40,000	$ 3,800	22%
$ 40,000	$ 60,000	$ 8,200	24%
$ 60,000	$ 80,000	$ 13,000	26%
$ 80,000	$ 100,000	$ 18,200	28%
$ 100,000	$ 150,000	$ 23,800	30%
$ 150,000	$ 250,000	$ 38,800	32%
$ 250,000	$ 500,000	$ 70,800	34%
$ 500,000	$ 750,000	$ 155,800	37%
$ 750,000	$ 1,000,000	$ 248,300	39%
$ 1,000,000	$ 1,250,000	$ 345,800	41%
$ 1,250,000	$ 1,500,000	$ 448,300	43%
$ 1,500,000	$ 2,000,000	$ 555,800	45%
$ 2,000,000	$ 2,500,000	$ 780,800	49%
$ 2,500,000	$ 3,000,000	$1,025,800	53%
$ 3,000,000	$10,000,000	$1,290,800	55%
$10,000,000	$17,184,000	$5,140,800	60%
$17,184,000		$9,451,200	55%

Year	Credit	Exemption Equivalent
2000-01	$220,550	$ 675,000
2002-03	$229,800	$ 700,000
2004	$287,300	$ 850,000
2005	$326,300	$ 950,000
2006	$345,800	$1,000,000

CHAPTER 12
NEVADA FOR UNDER $350!

It is possible to incorporate your business on your own. While you will still need the services of a resident agent such as Nevada Corporate Headquarters, Inc. if you do not have a physical location in Nevada already you can still incorporate for under $250. The following are the fees that are associated with incorporating in Nevada:

Nevada State Filing Fee: $125 (One time fee)

This fee pays to have your Articles of Incorporation filed with the Secretary of State and the ability to have a value of $25,000 of stock. It is recommended to set up the Articles of Incorporation with 25,000,000 shares at $.001 par value, authorized for issue. This is equivalent to $25,000. If you need a certified copy it is an additional $10, and if you need to have the filing expedited in 24 hours it is an additional $50.

Nevada State Officer/Director Filing: $85 (Annually)

The list of officers is filed with the Secretary of State as public record. This is the only document that indicates the president, secretary, treasurer and director of the company. The fee and list are filed annually.

Resident Agent Fee: $100 and up (Annually)

If you do not have a physical location in the state of Nevada you will need the services of a resident agent, which is required by Nevada statutes.

The resident agent will file your Articles of Incorporation and Officer/Director list with the Secretary of State for a fee, or you can file the paperwork on your own. The steps needed to file with the State of Nevada are as follows:

STEP BY STEP
ON HOW TO INCORPORATE IN NEVADA:

STEP #1:

Customize the Articles of Incorporation in this book to your specifications. You will need to change the name of the corporation, address, incorporator and any other information you feel is necessary.

STEP #2:

Call Nevada Corporate Headquarters, Inc. at 800-398-1077 and ask for an Acceptance of Resident Agent form to be faxed to you. This is a document that needs to be filed with the Articles of Incorporation.

STEP #3:

Send the Articles of Incorporation, Acceptance of Resident Agent form and a check to the Secretary of State of Nevada for $125 and add $10 for certified copy and $50 for expedite. The address of where to send this is, Secretary of State (Carson), 101 North Carson Street, Suite 3, Carson City, NV 89701-4786. You may phone them at 775-684-5708 or fax 775-684-5725.

STEP #4:

You may call Nevada Corporate Headquarters and order a corporate record book with forms and stock certificates. When the Secretary of State files your Articles, they will send back a Corporate Charter. This is the corporation's birth certificate. You will place this document in the record book and add any additional information as you see fit.

The following are examples of necessary documentation for a corporation. These are Articles of Incorporation and Bylaws for a Nevada corporation. The first meeting minutes are standard for use with any corporation. The bank resolution is an example of what type of documentation is needed to record the activities of the corporation.

ARTICLES OF INCORPORATION OF

_____

a Nevada Corporation

I, the undersigned, being the original incorporator herein named, for the purpose of forming a Corporation under the General Corporation Laws of the State of Nevada, to do business both within and without the State of Nevada, do make and file these Articles of Incorporation, hereby declaring and certifying that the facts herein stated are true:

ARTICLE I

NAME

The name of the Corporation is _____

ARTICLE II

RESIDENT AGENT & REGISTERED OFFICE

Section 2.01. Resident Agent. The name and address of the Resident Agent for service of process is Nevada Corporate Headquarters, Inc., 5300 West Sahara, Suite 101, Las Vegas, Nevada 89146. Mailing Address: P.O. Box 27740, Las Vegas, NV 89126.

Section 2.02. Registered Office. The address of its Registered Office is 5300 West Sahara, Suite 101, Las Vegas, Nevada 89146.

Section 2.03. Other Offices. The Corporation may also maintain offices for the transaction of any business at such other places within or without the State of Nevada as it may from time to time determine. Corporate business of every kind and nature may be conducted, and meetings of Directors and Stockholders held outside the State of Nevada with the same effect as if in the State of Nevada.

ARTICLE III

PURPOSE

The Corporation is organized for the purpose of engaging in any lawful activity, within or without the State of Nevada.

ARTICLE IV

SHARES OF STOCK

Section 4.01 <u>Number and Class</u>. The Corporation shall authorize the issuance of a single class of Capital Stock in the amount of twenty-five million (25,000,000) shares of Common Stock, at $.001 par value.

Notwithstanding the foregoing these Articles hereby vest the Board of Directors of the Corporation with such authority as may be necessary to prescribe such classes, series and numbers of each class or series of Stock. In addition the Board is hereby vested with such authority as may be necessary to prescribe the voting powers, designations, preferences, limitations, restrictions and relative rights of each class or series of Stock created. All classes of Stock may be issued from time to time without action by the Stockholders.

Section 4.02. <u>No Pre-emptive Rights</u>. Unless otherwise determined by the Board of Directors, holders of the Stock of the Corporation shall not have any preference, pre-emptive right, or right of subscription to acquire any shares of the Corporation authorized, issued or sold, or to be authorized, issued or sold, and convertible into shares of the Corporation, nor to any right of subscription thereto.

Section 4.03. <u>Non-Assess Ability of Shares</u>. The Shares of the Corporation, after the amount of the subscription price has been paid, in money, property, or services, as the Directors shall determine, shall not be subject to assessment to pay the debts of the Corporation, nor for any other purpose, and no Stock issued as fully paid shall ever be assessable or assessed, and the Articles of Incorporation shall not be amended in this particular.

ARTICLE V

DIRECTORS

Section 5.01. <u>Governing Board</u>. The members of the Governing Board of the Corporation shall be styled as Directors.

Section 5.02. <u>Initial Board of Directors</u>. The initial Board of Directors shall consist of not less than one (1), and not more than seven (7) members. The name and address of an initial member of the Board of Directors is as follows:

NAME   ADDRESS

_____

This individual shall serve as Director until the first annual meeting of the Stockholders or until his successor(s) shall have been elected and qualified.

Section 5.03. <u>Change in Number of Directors</u>. The number of Directors may be increased or decreased by a duly adopted amendment to the Bylaws of the Corporation.

ARTICLE VI

<u>INCORPORATOR</u>

The name and address of the incorporator is _____

ARTICLE VII

<u>PERIOD OF DURATION</u>

The Corporation is to have a perpetual existence.

ARTICLE VIII

<u>DIRECTORS' AND OFFICERS' LIABILITY</u>

A Director or Officer of the Corporation shall not be personally liable to this Corporation or its Stockholders for damages for breach of fiduciary duty as a Director or Officer, but this Article shall not eliminate or limit the liability of a Director or Officer for (i) acts or omissions which involve intentional misconduct, fraud or a knowing violation of law or (ii) the unlawful payment of distributions. Any repeal or modification of this Article by the Stockholders of the Corporation shall be prospective only, and shall not adversely affect any limitation on the personal liability of a Director or Officer of the Corporation for acts or omissions prior to such repeal or modification.

ARTICLE IX

<u>INDEMNITY</u>

Every person who was or is a party to, or is threatened to be made a party to, or is involved in any action, suit or proceeding, whether civil, criminal, administrative or investigative, by reason of the fact that he, or a person of whom he is the legal representative, is or was a Director or Officer of the Corporation, or is or was serving at the request of the Corporation as a Director or Officer of another Corporation, or as its representative in a partnership, joint venture, trust or other enterprise, shall be indemnified and held harmless to the fullest extent legally permissible under the laws of the State of Nevada from time to time against all expenses, liability and loss (including attorneys' fees, judgments, fines and amounts paid or to be paid in settlement) reasonably incurred or suffered by him in connection therewith. Such right of indemnification shall be a contract right which may be enforced in any manner desired by such person. The expenses of Officers and Directors incurred in defending a civil or criminal action, suit or proceeding must be paid by the Corporation as they are incurred and in advance of the final disposition of the action, suit or proceeding, upon receipt of an undertaking by or on behalf of the Director or Officer to repay the amount if it is ultimately determined by a court of competent jurisdiction that he is not entitled to be indemnified by the Corporation. Such right of indemnification shall not be exclusive of any other right which such Directors, Officers or representatives may have or hereafter acquire, and, without limiting the generality of such statement, they shall be entitled to their respective rights of indemnification under any bylaw, agreement, vote of Stockholders, provision of law, or otherwise, as well as their rights under this Article.

Without limiting the application of the foregoing, the Stockholders or Board of Directors may adopt bylaws from time to time with respect to indemnification, to provide at all times the fullest indemnification permitted by the laws of the State of Nevada, and may cause the Corporation to purchase and maintain insurance on behalf of any person who is or was a Director or Officer of the Corporation, or is or was serving at the request of the Corporation as Director or Officer of another Corporation, or as its representative in a partnership, joint venture, trust or other enterprises against any liability asserted against such person and incurred in any such capacity or arising out of such status, whether or not the Corporation would have the power to indemnify such person.

The indemnification provided in this Article shall continue as to a person who has ceased to be a Director, Officer, Employee or Agent, and shall inure to the benefit of the heirs, executors and administrators of such person.

ARTICLE X
AMENDMENTS

Subject at all times to the express provisions of Section 4.03 which cannot be amended, this Corporation reserves the right to amend, alter, change, or repeal any provision contained in these Articles of Incorporation or its Bylaws, in the manner now or hereafter prescribed by statute or by these Articles of Incorporation or said Bylaws, and all rights conferred upon the Stockholders are granted subject to this reservation.

ARTICLE XI
POWERS OF DIRECTORS

In furtherance and not in limitation of the powers conferred by statute the Board of Directors is expressly authorized:

(1) Subject to the Bylaws, if any, adopted by the Stockholders, to make, alter or repeal the Bylaws of the Corporation;

(2) To authorize and cause to be executed mortgages and liens, with or without limit as to amount, upon the real and personal property of the Corporation;

(3) To authorize the guaranty by the Corporation of securities, evidences of indebtedness and obligations of other persons, Corporations and business entities;

(4) To set apart out of any of the funds of the Corporation available for distributions a reserve or reserves for any proper purpose and to abolish any such reserve;

(5) By resolution, to designate one or more committees, each committee to consist of at least one Director of the Corporation, which, to the extent provided in the resolution or in the Bylaws of the Corporation, shall have and may exercise the powers of the Board of Directors in the management of the business and affairs of the Corporation, and may authorize the seal of the Corporation to be affixed to all papers which may require it. Such committee or committees shall have such name or names as may be stated in the Bylaws of the Corporation or as may be determined from time to time by resolution adopted by the Board of Directors; and

(6) To authorize the Corporation by its Officers or agents to exercise all such powers and to do all such acts and things as may be exercised or done by the Corporation, except and to the extent that any such statute shall require action by the Stockholders of the Corporation with regard to the exercising of any such power or the doing of any such act or thing.

In addition to the powers and authorities hereinbefore or by statute expressly conferred upon them, the Board of Directors may exercise all such powers and do all such acts and things as may be exercised or done by the Corporation, except as otherwise provided herein and by law.

IN WITNESS WHEREOF, I have hereunto set my hand this _____ day of _____, 2001, hereby declaring and certifying that the facts stated hereinabove are true.

_____

Signature of Incorporator

DEAN HELLER

Secretary of State

Telephone (702) 876-5203

Fax (702) 687-3471

STATE OF NEVADA

OFFICE OF THE SECRETARY OF STATE

State Capitol Complex

Carson City, Nevada 89710

CERTIFICATE OF ACCEPTANCE OF APPOINTMENT
BY
RESIDENT AGENT

In the matter of_____

I, <u>NEVADA CORPORATE HEADQUARTERS, INC.</u>, hereby state that on_____

I accepted the appointment as resident agent for the above named business entity.

The street address of the resident agent in this state is as follows:

5300 W. Sahara Avenue, Suite 101

Las Vegas, Nevada 89146

Date:_____

X_____

Cort W. Christie

(For Nevada Corporate Headquarters, Inc.)

BYLAWS

OF

_____

A Nevada Corporation

ARTICLE I

Stockholders

Section 1. <u>Annual Meeting</u>. Annual meetings of the Stockholders, commencing with the year _____shall be held on the_____day of _____each year if not a legal holiday and, if a legal holiday, then on the next secular day following, or at such other time as may be set by the Board of Directors from time to time, at which the Stockholders shall elect by vote a Board of Directors and transact such other business as may properly be brought before the meeting.

Section 2. <u>Special Meetings</u>. Special meetings of the Stockholders, for any purpose or purposes, unless otherwise prescribed by statute or by the Articles of Incorporation, may be called by the President or the Secretary by resolution of the Board of Directors or at the request in writing of Stockholders owning a majority in amount of the entire capital stock of the Corporation issued and outstanding and entitled to vote. Such request shall state the purpose of the proposed meeting.

Section 3. <u>Place of Meetings</u>. All annual meetings of the Stockholders shall be held at the registered office of the Corporation or at such other place within or without the State of Nevada as the Directors shall determine. Special meetings of the Stockholders may be held at such time and place within or without the State of Nevada as shall be stated in the notice of the meeting, or in a duly executed waiver of notice thereof. Business transacted at any special meeting of Stockholders shall be limited to the purposes stated in the notice.

Section 4. <u>Quorum; Adjourned Meetings</u>. The holders of a majority of the Stock issued and outstanding and entitled to vote thereat, present in person or represented by proxy, shall constitute a quorum at all meetings of the Stockholders for the transaction of business except as otherwise provided by statute or by the Articles of Incorporation. If, however, such quorum shall not be present or represented at any meeting of the Stockholders, the Stockholders entitled to vote thereat, present in person or represented by proxy, shall have the power to adjourn the meeting from time to time, without notice other than announcement at the meeting, until a quorum shall be present or represented. At such adjourned meeting at which a quorum shall be present or represented, any business may be transacted which might have been transacted at the meeting as originally notified.

Section 5. <u>Voting</u>. Each Stockholder of record of the Corporation holding Stock which is entitled to vote at this meeting shall be entitled at each meeting of Stockholders to one vote for each share of Stock standing in his name on the books of the Corporation. Upon the demand of any Stockholder, the vote for Directors and the vote upon any question before the meeting shall be by ballot.

When a quorum is present or represented at any meeting, the vote of the holders of a majority of the Stock having voting power present in person or represented by proxy shall be sufficient to elect Directors or to decide any question brought before such meeting, unless the question is one upon which by express provision of the statutes or of the Articles of Incorporation, a different vote is required in which case such express provision shall govern and control the decision of such question.

Section 6. <u>Proxies</u>. At any meeting of the Stockholders any Stockholder may be represented and vote by a proxy or proxies appointed by an instrument in writing. In the event that any such instrument in writing shall designate two or more persons to act as proxies, a majority of such persons present at the meeting, or, if only one shall be present, then that one shall have and may exercise all of the powers conferred by such written instrument upon all of the persons so designated unless the instrument shall otherwise provide. No proxy or power of attorney to vote shall be used to vote at a meeting of the Stockholders unless it shall have been filed with the secretary of the meeting. All questions regarding the qualification of voters, the validity of proxies and the acceptance or rejection of votes shall be decided by the inspectors of election who shall be appointed by the Board of Directors, or if not so appointed, then by the presiding Officer of the meeting.

Section 7. <u>Action Without Meeting</u>. Any action which may be taken by the vote of the Stockholders at a meeting may be taken without a meeting if authorized by the written consent of Stockholders holding at least a majority of the voting power, unless the provisions of the statutes or of the Articles of Incorporation require a greater proportion of voting power to authorize such action in which case such greater proportion of written consents shall be required.

ARTICLE II

Directors

Section 1. <u>Management of Corporation</u>. The business of the Corporation shall be managed by its Board of Directors which may exercise all such powers of the Corporation and do all such lawful acts and things as are not by statute or by the Articles of Incorporation or by these Bylaws directed or required to be exercised or done by the Stockholders.

Section 2. <u>Number, Tenure, and Qualifications</u>. The number of Directors which shall constitute the whole board shall be at least one. The number of Directors may from time to time be increased or decreased to not less than one nor more than fifteen. The Directors shall be elected at the annual meeting of the Stockholders and except as provided in Section 2 of this Article, each Director elected shall hold office until his successor is elected and qualified. Directors need not be Stockholders.

Section 3. <u>Vacancies</u>. Vacancies in the Board of Directors including those caused by an increase in the number of Directors, may be filled by a majority of the remaining Directors, though less than a quorum, or by a sole remaining Director, and each Director so elected shall hold office until his successor is elected at an annual or a special meeting of the Stockholders. The holders of two-thirds of the outstanding shares of Stock entitled to vote may at any time peremptorily terminate the term of office of all or any of the Directors by vote at a meeting called for such purpose or by a written statement filed with the secretary or, in his absence, with any other Officer. Such removal shall be effective immediately, even if successors are not elected simultaneously.

A vacancy or vacancies in the Board of Directors shall be deemed to exist in case of the death, resignation or removal of any Directors, or if the authorized number of Directors be increased, or if the Stockholders fail at any annual or special meeting of Stockholders at which any Director or Directors are elected to elect the full authorized number of Directors to be voted for at that meeting.

If the Board of Directors accepts the resignation of a Director tendered to take effect at a future time, the Board or the Stockholders shall have power to elect a successor to take office when the resignation is to become effective.

No reduction of the authorized number of Directors shall have the effect of removing any Director prior to the expiration of his term of office.

Section 4. <u>Annual and Regular Meetings</u>. Regular meetings of the Board of Directors shall be held at any place within or without the State which has been designated from time to time by resolution of the Board or by written consent of all members of the Board. In the absence of such designation regular meetings shall be held at the registered office of the Corporation. Special meetings of the Board may be held either at a place so designated or at the registered office.

Regular meetings of the Board of Directors may be held without call or notice at such time and at such place as shall from time to time be fixed and determined by the Board of Directors.

Section 5. <u>First Meeting</u>. The first meeting of each newly elected Board of Directors shall be held immediately following the adjournment of the meeting of Stockholders and at the place thereof. No notice of such meeting shall be necessary to the Directors in order legally to constitute the meeting, provided a quorum be present. In the event such meeting is not so held, the meeting may be held at such time and place as shall be specified in a notice given as hereinafter provided for special meetings of the Board of Directors.

Section 6. <u>Special Meetings</u>. Special meetings of the Board of Directors may be called by the Chairman or the President or by any Vice President or by any two Directors.

Written notice of the time and place of special meetings shall be delivered personally to each Director, or sent to each Director by mail or by other form of written communication, charges prepaid, addressed to him at his address as it is shown upon the records or if such address is not readily ascertainable, at the place in which the meetings of the Directors are regularly held. In case such notice is mailed or telegraphed, it shall be deposited in the United States mail or delivered to the telegraph company at least three (3) days prior to the time of the holding of the meeting. In case such notice is hand delivered as above provided, it shall be so delivered at least twenty-four (24) hours prior to the time of the holding of the meeting. Such mailing, telegraphing or delivery as above provided shall be due, legal and personal notice to such Director.

Section 7. <u>Business of Meetings</u>. The transactions of any meeting of the Board of Directors, however called and noticed or wherever held, shall be as valid as though had at a meeting duly held after regular call and notice, if a quorum be present, and if, either before or after the meeting, each of the Directors not present signs a written waiver of notice, or a consent to holding such meeting, or an approval of the minutes thereof. All such waivers, consents or approvals shall be filed with the corporate records or made a part of the minutes of the meeting.

Section 8. <u>Quorum; Adjourned Meetings</u>. A majority of the authorized number of Directors shall be necessary to constitute a quorum for the transaction of business, except to adjourn as hereinafter provided. Every act or decision done or made by a majority of the Directors present at a meeting duly held at which a quorum is present shall be regarded as the act of the Board of Directors, unless a greater number be required by law or by the Articles of Incorporation. Any action of a majority, although not at a regularly called meeting, and the record thereof, if assented to in writing by all of the other members of the Board shall be as valid and effective in all respects as if passed by the Board in regular meeting.

A quorum of the Directors may adjourn any Directors meeting to meet again at a stated day and hour; provided, however, that in the absence of a quorum, a majority of the Directors present at any Directors meeting, either regular or special, may adjourn from time to time until the time fixed for the next regular meeting of the Board.

Notice of the time and place of holding an adjourned meeting need not be given to the absent Directors if the time and place be fixed at the meeting adjourned.

Section 9. <u>Committees</u>. The Board of Directors may, by resolution adopted by a majority of the whole Board, designate one or more committees of the Board of Directors, each committee to consist of at least one or more of the Directors of the Corporation which, to the extent provided in the resolution, shall have and may exercise the power of the Board of Directors in the management of the business and affairs of the Corporation and may have power to authorize the seal of the Corporation to be affixed to all papers which may require it.

Such committee or committees shall have such name or names as may be determined from time to time by the Board of Directors. The members of any such committee present at any meeting and not disqualified from voting may, whether or not they constitute a quorum, unanimously appoint another member of the Board of Directors to act at the meeting in the place of any absent or disqualified member. At meetings of such committees, a majority of the members or alternate members shall constitute a quorum for the transaction of business, and the act of a majority of the members or alternate members at any meeting at which there is a quorum shall be the act of the committee.

The committees shall keep regular minutes of their proceedings and report the same to the Board of Directors.

Section 10. Action Without Meeting. Any action required or permitted to be taken at any meeting of the Board of Directors or of any committee thereof may be taken without a meeting if a written consent thereto is signed by all members of the Board of Directors or of such committee, as the case may be, and such written consent is filed with the minutes of proceedings of the Board or committee.

Section 11. Special Compensation. The Directors may be paid their expenses of attendance at each meeting of the Board of Directors and may be paid a fixed sum for attendance at each meeting of the Board of Directors or a stated salary as Director. No such payment shall preclude any Director from serving the Corporation in any other capacity and receiving compensation therefor. Members of special or standing committees may be allowed like reimbursement and compensation for attending committee meetings.

ARTICLE III

Notices

Section 1. Notice of Meetings. Notices of meetings shall be in writing and signed by the President or a Vice President or the Secretary or an Assistant Secretary or by such other person or persons as the Directors shall designate. Such notice shall state the purpose or purposes for which the meeting is called and the time and the place, which may be within or without this State, where it is to be held. A copy of such notice shall be either delivered personally to or shall be mailed, postage prepaid, to each Stockholder of record entitled to vote at such meeting not less than ten (10) nor more than sixty (60) days before such meeting. If mailed, it shall be directed to a Stockholder at his address as it appears upon the records of the Corporation and upon such mailing of any such notice, the service thereof shall be complete and the time of the notice shall begin to run from the date upon which such notice is deposited in the mail for transmission to such Stockholder. Personal delivery of any such notice to any Officer of a Corporation or association, or to any member of a partnership shall constitute delivery of such notice to such Corporation, association or partnership. In the event of the transfer of

Stock after delivery of such notice of and prior to the holding of the meeting it shall not be necessary to deliver or mail notice of the meeting to the transferee.

Section 2. <u>Effect of Irregularly Called Meetings</u>. Whenever all parties entitled to vote at any meeting, whether of Directors or Stockholders, consent, either by a writing on the records of the meeting or filed with the Secretary, or by presence at such meeting and oral consent entered on the minutes, or by taking part in the deliberations at such meeting without objection, the doings of such meeting shall be as valid as if had at a meeting regularly called and noticed, and at such meeting any business may be transacted which is not excepted from the written consent or to the consideration of which no objection for want of notice is made at the time, and if any meeting be irregular for want of notice or of such consent, provided a quorum was present at such meeting, the proceedings of said meeting may be ratified and approved and rendered likewise valid and the irregularity or defect therein waived by a writing signed by all parties having the right to vote at such meeting; and such consent or approval of Stockholders may be by proxy or attorney, but all such proxies and powers of attorney must be in writing.

Section 3. <u>Waiver of Notice</u>. Whenever any notice whatever is required to be given under the provisions of the statutes, of the Articles of Incorporation or of these Bylaws, a waiver thereof in writing, signed by the person or persons entitled to said notice, whether before or after the time stated therein, shall be deemed equivalent thereto.

ARTICLE IV

Officers

Section 1. <u>Election</u>. The Officers of the Corporation shall be chosen by the Board of Directors and shall be a President, a Secretary and a Treasurer, none of whom need be Directors. Any person may hold two or more offices. The Board of Directors may appoint a Chairman of the Board, Vice Chairman of the Board, one or more Vice Presidents, Assistant Treasurers and Assistant Secretaries.

Section 2. <u>Chairman of the Board</u>. The Chairman of the Board shall preside at meetings of the Stockholders and the Board of Directors, and shall see that all orders and resolutions of the Board of Directors are carried into effect.

Section 3. <u>Vice Chairman of the Board</u>. The Vice Chairman shall, in the absence or disability of the Chairman of the Board, perform the duties and exercise the powers of the Chairman of the Board and shall perform such other duties as the Board of Directors may from time to time prescribe.

Section 4. <u>President</u>. The President shall be the Chief Executive Officer of the Corporation and shall have active management of the business of the Corporation. He shall execute on behalf of the Corporation all instruments requiring such execution except to the extent the signing and execution thereof shall be expressly designated by the Board of Directors to some other Officer or agent of the Corporation.

Section 5. <u>Vice President.</u> The Vice President shall act under the direction of the President and in the absence or disability of the President shall perform the duties and exercise the powers of the President. They shall perform such other duties and have such other powers as the President or the Board of Directors may from time to time prescribe. The Board of Directors may designate one or more Executive Vice Presidents or may otherwise specify the order of seniority of the Vice Presidents. The duties and powers of the President shall descend to the Vice Presidents in such specified order of seniority.

Section 6. <u>Secretary.</u> The Secretary shall act under the direction of the President. Subject to the direction of the President he shall attend all meetings of the Board of Directors and all meetings of the Stockholders and record the proceedings. He shall perform like duties for the standing committees when required. He shall give, or cause to be given, notice of all meetings of the Stockholders and special meetings of the Board of Directors, and shall perform such other duties as may be prescribed by the President or the Board of Directors.

Section 7. <u>Assistant Secretaries.</u> The Assistant Secretaries shall act under the direction of the President. In order of their seniority, unless otherwise determined by the President or the Board of Directors, they shall, in the absence or disability of the Secretary, perform the duties and exercise the powers of the Secretary. They shall perform such other duties and have such other powers as the President or the Board of Directors may from time to time prescribe.

Section 8. <u>Treasurer.</u> The Treasurer shall act under the direction of the President. Subject to the direction of the President he shall have custody of the corporate funds and securities and shall keep full and accurate accounts of receipts and disbursements in books belonging to the Corporation and shall deposit all monies and other valuable effects in the name and to the credit of the Corporation in such depositories as may be designated by the Board of Directors. He shall disburse the funds of the Corporation as may be ordered by the President or the Board of Directors, taking proper vouchers for such disbursements, and shall render to the President and the Board of Directors, at its regular meetings, or when the Board of Directors so requires, an account of all his transactions as Treasurer and of the financial condition of the Corporation.

If required by the Board of Directors, he shall give the Corporation a bond in such sum and with such surety or sureties as shall be satisfactory to the Board of Directors for the faithful performance of the duties of his office and for the restoration to the Corporation, in case of his death, resignation, retirement or removal from office, of all books, papers, vouchers, money and other property of whatever kind in his possession or under his control belonging to the Corporation.

Section 9. <u>Assistant Treasurers.</u> The Assistant Treasurers in the order of their seniority, unless otherwise determined by the President or the Board of Directors, shall, in the absence or disability of the Treasurer, perform the duties and exercise the powers of the Treasurer. They shall perform such other duties and have such other powers as the President or the Board of Directors may from time to time prescribe.

Section 10. <u>Compensation</u>. The salaries and compensation of all Officers of the Corporation shall be fixed by the Board of Directors.

Section 11. <u>Removal; Resignation</u>. The Officers of the Corporation shall hold office at the pleasure of the Board of Directors. Any Officer elected or appointed by the Board of Directors may be removed at any time by the Board of Directors. Any vacancy occurring in any office of the Corporation by death, resignation, removal or otherwise shall be filled by the Board of Directors.

ARTICLE V

Capital Stock

Section 1. <u>Certificates</u>. Every Stockholder shall be entitled to have a certificate signed by the President or a Vice President and the Treasurer or an Assistant Treasurer, or the Secretary or an Assistant Secretary of the Corporation, certifying the number of shares owned by him in the Corporation. If the Corporation shall be authorized to issue more than one class of Stock or more than one series of any class, the designations, preferences and relative, participating, optional or other special rights of the various classes of Stock or series thereof and the qualifications, limitations or restrictions of such rights, shall be set forth in full or summarized on the face or back of the certificate, which the Corporation shall issue to represent such Stock.

If a certificate is signed (1) by a transfer agent other than the Corporation or its employees or (2) by a registrar other than the Corporation or its employees, the signatures of the Officers of the Corporation may be facsimiles. In case any Officer who has signed or whose facsimile signature has been placed upon a certificate shall cease to be such Officer before such certificate is issued, such certificate may be issued with the same effect as though the person had not ceased to be such Officer. The seal of the Corporation, or a facsimile thereof, may, but need not be, affixed to certificates of Stock.

Section 2. <u>Surrendered; Lost or Destroyed Certificates</u>. The Board of Directors may direct a new certificate or certificates to be issued in place of any certificate or certificates theretofore issued by the Corporation alleged to have been lost or destroyed upon the making of an affidavit of that fact by the person claiming the certificate of Stock to be lost or destroyed. When authorizing such issue of a new certificate or certificates, the Board of Directors may, in its discretion and as a condition precedent to the issuance thereof, require the owner of such lost or destroyed certificate or certificates, or his legal representative, to advertise the same in such manner as it shall require and/or give the Corporation a bond in such sum as it may direct as indemnity against any claim that may be made against the Corporation with respect to the certificate alleged to have been lost or destroyed.

Section 3. <u>Replacement Certificates</u>. Upon surrender to the Corporation or the transfer agent of the Corporation of a certificate for shares duly endorsed or accompanied by proper evidence of succession, assignment or authority to transfer, it shall be the duty of the Corporation, if it is satisfied that all provisions of the laws and regulations applicable to the Corporation regarding transfer and ownership of shares have been complied with, to issue a new certificate to the person entitled thereto, cancel the old certificate and record the transaction upon its books.

Section 4. <u>Record Date</u>. The Board of Directors may fix in advance a date not exceeding sixty (60) days nor less than ten (10) days preceding the date of any meeting of Stockholders, or the date for the payment of any distribution, or the date for the allotment of rights, or the date when any change or conversion or exchange of capital Stock shall go into effect, or a date in connection with obtaining the consent of Stockholders for any purpose, as a record date for the determination of the Stockholders entitled to notice of and to vote at any such meeting, and any adjournment thereof, or entitled to receive payment of any such distribution, or to give such consent, and in such case, such Stockholders, and only such Stockholders as shall be Stockholders of record on the date so fixed, shall be entitled to notice of and to vote at such meeting, or any adjournment thereof, or to receive payment of such distribution, or to receive such allotment of rights, or to exercise such rights, or to give such consent, as the case may be, notwithstanding any transfer of any Stock on the books of the Corporation after any such record date fixed as aforesaid.

Section 5. <u>Registered Owner</u>. The Corporation shall be entitled to recognize the person registered on its books as the owner of shares to be the exclusive owner for all purposes including voting and distribution, and the Corporation shall not be bound to recognize any equitable or other claim to or interest in such share or shares on the part of any other person, whether or not it shall have express or other notice thereof, except as otherwise provided by the laws of Nevada.

ARTICLE VI

General Provisions

Section 1. <u>Registered Office</u>. The registered office of this Corporation shall be in the County of Clark, State of Nevada. The Corporation may also have offices at such other places both within and without the State of Nevada as the Board of Directors may from time to time determine or the business of the Corporation may require.

Section 2. <u>Distributions</u>. Distributions upon capital stock of the Corporation, subject to the provisions of the Articles of Incorporation, if any, may be declared by the Board of Directors at any regular or special meeting, pursuant to law. Distributions may be paid in cash, in property or in shares of capital stock, subject to the provisions of the Articles of Incorporation.

Section 3. <u>Reserves</u>. Before payment of any distribution, there may be set aside out of any funds of the Corporation available for distributions such sum or sums as the Directors from time to time, in their absolute discretion, think proper as a reserve or reserves to meet contingencies, or for equalizing distributions or for repairing or maintaining any property of the Corporation or for such other purpose as the Directors shall think conducive to the interest of the Corporation, and the Directors may modify or abolish any such reserve in the manner in which it was created.

Section 4. <u>Checks; Notes</u>. All checks or demands for money and notes of the Corporation shall be signed by such Officer or Officers or such other person or persons as the Board of Directors may from time to time designate.

Section 5. <u>Fiscal Year</u>. The fiscal year of the Corporation shall be fixed by resolution of the Board of Directors.

Section 6. <u>Corporate Seal</u>. The Corporation may or may not have a corporate seal, as may from time to time be determined by resolution of the Board of Directors. If a corporate seal is adopted, it shall have inscribed thereon the name of the Corporation and the words "Corporate Seal" and "Nevada". The seal may be used by causing it or a facsimile thereof to be impressed or affixed or in any manner reproduced.

ARTICLE VII

Indemnification

Section 1. <u>Indemnification of Officers and Directors, Employees and Other Persons</u>. Every person who was or is a party or is threatened to be made a party to or is involved in any action, suit or proceeding, whether civil, criminal, administrative or investigative, by reason of the fact that he or a person of whom he is the legal representative is or was a Director or Officer of the Corporation or is or was serving at the request of the Corporation or for its benefit as a Director or Officer of another Corporation, or as its representative in a partnership, joint venture, trust or other enterprise, shall be indemnified and held harmless to the fullest extent legally permissible under the general Corporation law of the State of Nevada from time to time against all expenses, liability and loss (including attorneys' fees, judgments, fines and amounts paid or to be paid in settlement) reasonably incurred or suffered by him in connection therewith. The expenses of Officers and Directors incurred in defending a civil or criminal action, suit or proceeding must be paid by the Corporation as they are incurred and in advance of the final disposition of the action, suit or proceeding upon receipt of an undertaking by or on behalf of the Director or Officer to repay the amount if it is ultimately determined by a court of competent jurisdiction that he is not entitled to be indemnified by the Corporation. Such right of indemnification shall be a contract right which may be enforced in any manner desired by such person. Such right of indemnification shall not be exclusive of any other right which such Directors, Officers or representatives may have or hereafter acquire and, without limiting the generality of such statement, they shall be entitled to their respective rights of indemnification under any bylaw, agreement, vote of Stockholders, provision of law or otherwise, as well as their rights under this Article.

Section 2. <u>Insurance</u>. The Board of Directors may cause the Corporation to purchase and maintain insurance on behalf of any person who is or was a Director or Officer of the Corporation, or is or was serving at the request of the Corporation as a Director or Officer of another Corporation, or as its representative in a partnership, joint venture, trust or other enterprise against any liability asserted against such person and incurred in any such capacity or arising out of such status, whether or not the Corporation would have the power to indemnify such person.

Section 3. <u>Further Bylaws</u>. The Board of Directors may from time to time adopt further Bylaws with respect to indemnification and may amend these and such Bylaws to provide at all times the fullest indemnification permitted by the General Corporation Law of the State of Nevada.

ARTICLE VIII

Amendments

Section 1. <u>Amendments by Stockholders</u>. The Bylaws may be amended by a majority vote of all the Stock issued and outstanding and entitled to vote for the election of Directors of the Stockholders, provided notice of intention to amend shall have been contained in the notice of the meeting.

Section 2. <u>Amendments by Board of Directors</u>. The Board of Directors by a majority vote of the whole Board at any meeting may amend these Bylaws, including Bylaws adopted by the Stockholders, but the Stockholders may from time to time specify particular provisions of the Bylaws, which shall not be amended by the Board of Directors.

APPROVED AND ADOPTED this_____day of_____, 20____.

X_____(Sign)

SECRETARY

CERTIFICATE OF SECRETARY

I hereby certify that I am the Secretary of _____and that the foregoing Bylaws, constitute the code of Bylaws of_____as duly adopted at a regular meeting of the Board of Directors of the Corporation.

DATED this_____day of_____, 20_____.

X_____(**Sign**)

SECRETARY

(***BANK RESOLUTION***)
RESOLUTION OF THE BOARD OF DIRECTORS OF

I, _____ the undersigned, Secretary of
a Nevada Corporation, do hereby certify that:

NAME	TITLE	SIGNATURE
(Print Name)		*(Sign)*

X _____ the PRES.   who *signs* X _____

X _____ the V.P.   who *signs* X _____

X _____ the SEC.   who *signs* X _____

X _____ the TRES.   who *signs* X _____

X _____ the AGENT   who *signs* X _____

are the present Officers of this Corporation.

RESOLVED, that any one Officer is authorized to establish bank accounts, effect loan transactions, purchase and sell real and/or personal property, negotiate mortgages, options and any other instruments necessary and/or useful to the operation of a general and/or manufacturing business without limit as to amount and upon such terms as they shall deem fit. Only one signature will be required to bind the Corporation; the Corporation hereby ratifies and confirms any and all previous acts of these Officers as though such acts had been completed after the effective date of this resolution.

FURTHER RESOLVED, that the authority herein conferred shall continue until revoked by the Board of Directors of this Corporation.

I,_____, do hereby certify that I am the duly elected and qualified Secretary and keeper of the records of this Corporation, and that the above is a true and correct copy of a resolution duly adopted at a meeting of the Board of Directors thereof, convened and held in accordance with the laws of the State of Nevada and the Bylaws of said Corporation on this_____day of _____, _____, and that such resolution is now in full force and effect.

X_____(Sign)

SECRETARY

MINUTES OF
FIRST MEETING OF BOARD OF DIRECTORS

The First Meeting of the Board of Directors of_____ a Nevada Corporation, convened on the _____ day of _____, _____, pursuant to waiver of notice and consent to the holding thereof executed by each Director of the Corporation. Present were all the Directors:

_____was elected temporary Chairman of the Board and _____was elected temporary Secretary, each to serve only until the close of the meeting.

The Chairman reported that the Articles of Incorporation of the Corporation had been filed in the Office of the Nevada Secretary of State on the_____day of _____and that as a consequence, the Corporation is duly and validly existing and in good standing under the laws of the State of Nevada and qualified to proceed with the transactions of business. The Certificate of Incorporation of the Corporation then being exhibited, on motion duly made, seconded and carried, said Certificate of Incorporation was accepted and approved.

The Secretary presented a proposed form of Bylaws for the regulation and management of the affairs of the Corporation. The Bylaws were read and considered, and upon motion duly made, seconded and carried, were adopted and ordered filed with the minutes of the meeting.

On motion duly made, seconded and carried, the Directors were recognized as the first Directors of the Corporation and it was further moved that they were to hold office until the first annual meeting of shareholders or until their respective successors shall be duly elected and qualified.

The Chairman called for the nomination of Officers of the Corporation. Thereupon, the following persons were nominated for the Officers of the Corporation:

(Print Names)

PRESIDENT: _____

VICE PRESIDENT: _____

SECRETARY: _____

TREASURER: _____

No further nominations being made the nominations were closed and the Directors proceeded to vote on the nominees. All of the Directors present at the meeting having voted and the vote having been counted, the Chairman announced the aforesaid nominees had been duly elected to the offices set before their respective names. The permanent Officers of the Corporation then took charge of the meeting.

Upon motion duly made, seconded and carried, the following resolutions were adopted:

RESOLVED, that the specific form (List of Officers, Directors and Agent of) of resolutions appointing the Resident Agent and specifying the principal place of business supplied by the Nevada Secretary of State be and is hereby adopted as the official resolutions and list of this Corporation.

RESOLVED, that the Treasurer be and is hereby authorized to pay all fees and expenses incident to and necessary for the organization of this Corporation.

RESOLVED, that the proper Officers of this Corporation be and they hereby are authorized and directed on behalf of the Corporation, to make and file such certificates, reports, or other instruments as may be required by law to be filed in any State in which said Officers shall find it necessary or expedient to file the same to register or authorize the Corporation to transact business in such State.

RESOLVED, that the treasurer be and is hereby ordered to open a bank, and or brokerage account in the name of this Corporation as appropriate for deposit of funds belonging to the Corporation, such funds to be withdrawn only be check of the Corporation signed by its President and/or any one, unless changed by resolution, authorized individual.

RESOLVED, a form of Stock Certificate was presented, examined, approved and duly adopted for use by the Corporation. Certificate No. 00 was directed to be inserted in the Corporate Record Book as evidence and sample thereof.

RESOLVED, that the Board of Directors of this Corporation deem it desirable and/or prudent to, from time to time, utilize an official corporate seal (optional under Nevada law) and, therefore, that the corporate seal presented to this Board, circular in form with the inscription of the corporate name, _____, and the official date of Incorporation, be, and the same hereby is adopted as the official seal of the Corporation, and be it

FURTHER RESOLVED, that the impression of said seal be made upon Certificate No. 00 inserted in the Corporate Record Book as evidence and sample thereof.

RESOLVED, that the fiscal year of the Corporation shall end on Last Day of the Month preceding _____, and commence on First Day of the _____, of each year hereafter.

FURTHER RESOLVED, that NEVADA CORPORATE HEADQUARTERS, INC., be, and hereby is appointed Resident Agent of this Corporation, in charge of the principal office, and so authorized to discharge the duties of Resident Agent, and be it.

FURTHER RESOLVED, that the Secretary forthwith supply a List of Officers and Directors to the Resident Agent for filing with the Secretary of State of the State of Nevada as required by law. (In the event the filing has not yet been accomplished), and be it

FURTHER RESOLVED, that the Secretary forthwith supply the Resident Agent with a certified copy of the Corporation Bylaws and a Stock Ledger Statement to be kept on file at the principal office as required by Nevada law. (In the event this has not yet been done.)

There being no other business to be transacted, the meeting was, upon motion duly made, seconded and carried, adjourned.

X _____ (Sign)
SECRETARY

CHAPTER 13
GLOSSARY OF TERMS

Alter Ego	"Other Self", a person who is legally the same as, and interchangeable with, another (e.g., the principal).
Articles of Incorporation	A formal document that creates a corporation; a charter.
Board of Directors	Group, elected by shareholders, to oversee the management of the corporation.
Bylaws	A rule adopted by an organization chiefly for the government of its members and the regulation of its affairs.
Charter	A formal document that creates a corporation; articles of incorporation.
"C" Corporation	A corporation that pays tax on its own income under the general rules of Subchapter C of the Internal Revenue Code.
Capital Stock	The outstanding shares of a joint-stock company considered as an aggregate.
Closely Held Company	A company whose shares are held mostly by a small group of investors, management, founders, and / or families.

Common Stock	All capital stock except for preferred stock.
Controlled Group	A group of corporations which are grouped together for one tax purpose or another. Control may be through parent-subsidiary relationships or common control, such as a brother-sister controlled group. Control means ownership of a certain percentage (generally, either at least 80% or less frequently, at least 50% of the total combined voting power of all classes of voting stock or of the total value of shares.
Corporation	A body formed and authorized by law to act as a single person although constituted by one or more persons and legally endowed with various rights and duties including the capacity of succession.
Director	A person elected by the shareholders to oversee the management of a corporation.
Double Taxation	Taxation by the federal government of corporate earnings once at the corporate level and again at the shareholder level upon distribution of dividends.
Encumbrance	A burden on either title to property or on the property itself (e.g., a mortgage, a lien).
Foreign Corporation	A corporation carrying on business in any state other than the state of its creation; in all such states, it is "foreign."
Fraudulent Conveyance	A contractual misrepresentation of the nature, quality, or existence of transferred assets. Also, a term denoting potential risk for sellers and lenders.
General Partnership	A partnership in which there are no limited partners, and each partner has managerial power and untitled liability for partnership debts.
Judgment Proof	Having few, if any, assets that can be reached by a judgment creditor; thus, persons against whom money judgments are of no practical effect.
Limited Liability	Liability (as a stockholder) limited by statute or treaty.

Par Value Stock	Stock for which a specified dollar amount is indicated on the share certificate; the par value must be set out in the charter.
Partnership	The association of two or more persons who have expressly or implicitly agreed to carry on, as co-owners, a business for profit.
Passive Income	Income to certain taxpayers (including: "S" corporation shareholders) that is subject to the passive activity loss (PAL) rules because the taxpayer does not materially participate in the business activity producing the income. Generally includes receipts from royalties, rents, dividends, interest, annuities, and the sale and exchange of stock and securities.
Preferred Stock	Stock guaranteed priority by a corporation's charter over common stock in the payment dividends and usually in the distribution of assets.
Pierce the Corporate Veil	To disregard the corporate entity, and thus hold the shareholders liable for corporate actions; this is possible under circumstances involving fraud.
"S" Corporation	A corporation that is eligible, and does elect to be taxed under the Subchapter S of the Internal Revenue Code. Basically, shareholders pay tax on the corporation's income by reporting their pro rate shares of pass-through items on their own individual income tax returns.
Professional Corporation	A corporation created by a professional or professionals in order to gain corporate tax advantages for traditional partnership or proprietary activities.
Resident Agent	A person or other entity authorized to receive service of process and other official papers for a corporation.
Shareholder	An owner of a share in a corporation through the ownership of its stock.
Sole Proprietorship	The simplest form of business in which a sole owner and his business are not legally distinct entities; the owner is personally liable for business debts.

| Stock | A share; also, the physical evidence of share ownership, the share certificate; also, the aggregate of corporate shares. |
| Stock Certificate | An instrument evidencing ownership of one or more shares of the capital stock of a corporation. |

CHAPTER 14
USEFUL WEBSITES

www.nchinc.com   Nevada Corporate Headquarters, Inc. website. A resident agent in Nevada.

www.corporatemanagercd.com   An interactive Corporate Resolution software program to maintain your corporate records.

www.corporateseminars.net   A list of several seminars for learning the secrets of operating a corporation.

www.agedcorporations.com   A site discussing the advantages of owning an aged or shelf corporation.

www.promotional-concepts.com   A list of business opportunities available on the internet.

www.bizavings.com   This site has various products available for educating small business owners.

www.incanywhere.com   Incorporates companies in any state.

www.corpensation.com   Discusses the benefits of setting up a retirement account for the corporation.

www.sos.state.nv.us	Nevada Secretary of State website.
www.shelfcorps.com	Specialty site for aged corporations.
www.creditandcommerce.net	Information on building corporate credit.
www.relocatenevada.com	Information for relocating to Nevada.
www.entitystructures.com	Discusses the advantages of using various entities with a Nevada Corporation.
www.incbookstore.com	An affiliate of Amazon.com, featuring business books for the business owner.
www.ideavirus.com	An Internet marketing site.
www.hostingwebsite.net	A web hosting and design company.
www.inc.com	Inc. magazine's website.
www.tele-direct.com	800# Web-enabled order-taking telephone call center specializing in response, e-commerce, direct mail, catalog order taking and credit card processing with live operators 24/7.
www.openair.com	Web-based professional services and management solutions that include time sheets, expense reports, project management, proposal writing and client invoicing.
www.000domains.com	Register your domain names here, for less.
www.ecxusa.com	Apply for an e-commerce merchant account here.
www.onebox.com	Free service providing phone, fax and email.
www.tamtam.com	Unleash your business internationally.
www.bizland.com	Free web services for your business.
www.ibizhome.com	Free business newsletters.

www.marketingtips.com	Some of the best internet marketing ideas.
www.buyerzone.com	Compare quotes on business products and services from name-brand vendors in your area.
www.findaccountingsoftware.com	Find the perfect accounting software for your business.
www.business-supply.com	Online catalog of over 20,000 brand name and discount computer and office supplies.
www.capitalsearch.com	Access business capital from private angel investors and venture capital sources.
www.smallbusinessloan.com	Two minute approval on your small business loan or equipment lease.
www.1trainingcenter.com	Over 370 web-based computer training courses.
www.buyingavenues.com	Localized business to business e-marketplace serving small businesses.
www.design-a-card.com	Design and order professionally printed business cards online.
www.roi.net	Creating a business, marketing, product or strategic plan.
www.instantsalesletters.com	Now in two minutes you can quickly and easily create a sales letter guaranteed to sell your product or service.
www.dnb-usa.com	Dun & Bradstreet – the leading provider of international and US business information.
www.careervoyager.com	The job search, career management and education portal.
www.businessnation.com	Business marketplace – bid, buy, sell, negotiate, barter in business product auctions.

To be added to an email list with special offers about Incorporating in Nevada, email **nchinc@nchinc.com**, with the subject (add to email list).

PRST STD
U.S. Paid Postage
PAID
Las Vegas, NV
Permit No. 170

BUSINESS REPLY MAIL
FIRST-CLASS MAIL   PERMIT NO. 170   LAS VEGAS NV

POSTAGE WILL BE PAID BY ADDRESSEE

NEVADA CORPORATE HEADQUARTERS, INC.
5300 W. Sahara Ave. Suite 100
Las Vegas, NV 89146

PRST STD
U.S. Paid Postage
PAID
Las Vegas, NV
Permit No. 170

BUSINESS REPLY MAIL
FIRST-CLASS MAIL   PERMIT NO. 170   LAS VEGAS NV

POSTAGE WILL BE PAID BY ADDRESSEE

NEVADA CORPORATE HEADQUARTERS, INC.
5300 W. Sahara Ave. Suite 100
Las Vegas, NV 89146

PRST STD
U.S. Paid Postage
PAID
Las Vegas, NV
Permit No. 170

BUSINESS REPLY MAIL
FIRST-CLASS MAIL   PERMIT NO. 170   LAS VEGAS NV

POSTAGE WILL BE PAID BY ADDRESSEE

NEVADA CORPORATE HEADQUARTERS, INC.
5300 W. Sahara Ave. Suite 100
Las Vegas, NV 89146

Nevada Corporate Headquarters, Inc.

○ **PLEASE CONTACT ME WITH MORE INFORMATION ON HOW I CAN INCORPORATE MY BUSINESS.**
Fill in the circle on which service or package you would like to know more about.

○ 24 Hour Classic Incorporation Service
○ Complete Resident Agent Services
○ Nevada Bank Account Set-Up
○ Mail Forwarding
○ Nevada Based Corporate Office Packages
○ Federal Tax Identification Number

○ Website Design
○ Logo Design
○ Domain Registration/Hosting
○ Corporate Express Package
○ Corporate Express Plus Package

○ Corporate Logic Package
○ Total Asset Protection Seminar
○ Corporate Fundamentals Seminar
○ Business Strategies Seminar
○ Tax Strategies Seminar

Name _____ Email _____
Address _____ City/State _____ Zip _____
Phone (Day) _____ (Evening) _____
Employer _____ Title _____

Call 1-800-398-1077 or visit www.nchinc.com for more information.

Nevada Corporate Headquarters, Inc.

○ **PLEASE CONTACT ME WITH MORE INFORMATION ON HOW I CAN INCORPORATE MY BUSINESS.**
Fill in the circle on which service or package you would like to know more about.

○ 24 Hour Classic Incorporation Service
○ Complete Resident Agent Services
○ Nevada Bank Account Set-Up
○ Mail Forwarding
○ Nevada Based Corporate Office Packages
○ Federal Tax Identification Number

○ Website Design
○ Logo Design
○ Domain Registration/Hosting
○ Corporate Express Package
○ Corporate Express Plus Package

○ Corporate Logic Package
○ Total Asset Protection Seminar
○ Corporate Fundamentals Seminar
○ Business Strategies Seminar
○ Tax Strategies Seminar

Name _____ Email _____
Address _____ City/State _____ Zip _____
Phone (Day) _____ (Evening) _____
Employer _____ Title _____

Call 1-800-398-1077 or visit www.nchinc.com for more information.

Nevada Corporate Headquarters, Inc.

○ **PLEASE CONTACT ME WITH MORE INFORMATION ON HOW I CAN INCORPORATE MY BUSINESS.**
Fill in the circle on which service or package you would like to know more about.

○ 24 Hour Classic Incorporation Service
○ Complete Resident Agent Services
○ Nevada Bank Account Set-Up
○ Mail Forwarding
○ Nevada Based Corporate Office Packages
○ Federal Tax Identification Number

○ Website Design
○ Logo Design
○ Domain Registration/Hosting
○ Corporate Express Package
○ Corporate Express Plus Package

○ Corporate Logic Package
○ Total Asset Protection Seminar
○ Corporate Fundamentals Seminar
○ Business Strategies Seminar
○ Tax Strategies Seminar

Name _____ Email _____
Address _____ City/State _____ Zip _____
Phone (Day) _____ (Evening) _____
Employer _____ Title _____

Call 1-800-398-1077 or visit www.nchinc.com for more information.